DATE DUE

HIGHSMITH   #45102

THE DRAGONSLAYER SERIES

OVERCOMING ANGER

& OTHER DRAGONS OF THE SOUL

Shaking Loose from Persistent Sins

Peter Wilkes

With Study Questions for
Individuals or Groups

INTERVARSITY PRESS
DOWNERS GROVE, ILLINOIS 60515

©1987 by InterVarsity Christian Fellowship

All rights reserved. No part of this book may be reproduced in any form without written permission from InterVarsity Press, P.O. Box 1400, Downers Grove, Illinois 60515.

InterVarsity Press is the book-publishing division of InterVarsity Christian Fellowship, a student movement active on campus at hundreds of universities, colleges and schools of nursing. For information about local and regional activities, write Public Relations Dept., InterVarsity Christian Fellowship, 6400 Schroeder Rd., P.O. Box 7895, Madison, WI 53707-7895.

Distributed in Canada through InterVarsity Press, 860 Denison St., Unit 3, Markham, Ontario L3R 4H1, Canada.

All Scripture quotations, unless otherwise indicated, are from the Holy Bible, New International Version. Copyright © 1973, 1978, International Bible Society. Used by permission of Zondervan Bible Publishers.

Cover photograph: Michael Goss

ISBN 0-87784-517-4

Printed in the United States of America

Library of Congress Cataloging-in-Publication Data

Wilkes, Peter, 1937-
  Overcoming anger and other dragons of the soul.

  (The DragonSlayer series)
  Bibliography: p.
  1. Vices. 2. Christian life—1960-   I. Title.
II. Series: DragonSlayer series.
BV4625.W55   1987   241'.3   87-3753
ISBN 0-87784-517-4

17	16	15	14	13	12	11	10	9	8	7	6	5	4	3	2	1
99	98	97	96	95	94	93	92	91	90	89	88	87				

To Norah,
dear companion of
my pilgrimage

Preface

If Christianity isn't practical, it's nothing. The writers of the New Testament were convinced that being a Christian makes a profound difference in the way we live. But they did not expect it to be easy. They frequently made urgent pleas to stand fast and to keep going.

This is a book to encourage you in the daily business of living as a Christian. I have deliberately emphasized the human side of the process because that is the part that is ours. Of course, we have behind us all the Father's power and his desire that we choose the right and do it. If I failed to acknowledge God's part in our lives, this would be merely a book of self-helps, not Christian at all. We desperately need to hear daily the enormous encouragement of his strengthening support.

I have not written much about God instantaneously removing problems of temptation. It's not that I don't believe in it. I have experienced it myself. Rather, I believe such miracles to be gracious exceptions. God is economical. He uses every experience to teach us. We learn about ourselves and our Father through struggles with temptation. Normally he helps us with our problems rather than removes them. If he has taken away a temptation that was dogging you, great! Be thankful. But do not expect it to happen all the time. As welcome as such relief is, it offers little help for those who have to take the long way around. This book is for such pilgrims.

I have learned about the way to win against temptation from three places. The Bible, that inexhaustible fount of practical wisdom, is my primary source. The second is my own struggle with the problems. I have faced all these dragons personally. The third source is my experience with the many people whose lives I have been privileged to share through counseling. They have shown me what can be accomplished by grace and by determination. You will meet some of them in these pages—with, of course, their names changed and details rearranged to preserve their anonymity. But they are not anonymous to me, and I thank them all for sharing their battles with me.

Introduction

A Guide to Dragon Slaying

Combat with dragons begins with the quest. We must find out where they live and breed. Unfortunately, we know where to find these dragons of evil all too easily. We just look within ourselves.

The landscape of our minds is occupied by enemies, dragons of all shapes and sizes. Some frighten us, puffing up to a vast size, breathing fire and smoke, blistering the paint work of our interior rooms with their acid breath. They are Guilt, Anger, Lust and Pride. Their aim is to intimidate us, to defeat us.

Other dragons are small and slimy. Their strategy is to undermine us. They leave a stench of disappointment in the air. Rarely meeting them face to face, we surprise them in dark corners, where we find they have already weakened us for the attack of their elder brother, Despair. They are Legalism, Doubt, Gossip and Laziness.

Are these dragons familiar? No doubt in your struggle for a whole and holy life you have met some of them already. Sometimes they work in concert. Experienced dragon fighters recognize that all these attacks are coordinated by an alien mind of great and threatening intelligence, the mind of the Dragon Maker.

Do not believe the lying whisper that either he or his ugly dragons are invincible. As you go questing for the evil creatures within, take the Christian's great weapon, the clear and shining light of God's true Word. In that light dragons shrink to a manageable size, and even the Dragon Maker himself is made vulnerable. You will understand the Dragon Maker's great secret: he has already been defeated by Jesus. His power is crumbling.

You have another tool for dragon slaying as well. You do not fight alone. Jesus has given you the greatest gift of all, his presence within you. As the Holy Spirit, God ensures your victory over dragons of all shapes and sizes.

You can live a whole and healthy Christian life. If you take your Christianity seriously, you will do all in your power to prepare for the warfare ahead. God has done his part. You can work at building your prayer life as a lifeline for power, you can search the Word, and you can join the fellowship of God's people. These three will be necessary no matter which dragon you face. The dragons are beatable. What follows in the rest of these pages will be practical strategies for recalcitrant dragons.

1
Overcoming Guilt

Finding Freedom in God's Justice

Jamie was a homosexual. He was also dying. His emaciated face stared out at me from my television screen, but it was his haunting voice that I remember.

"I'm guilty," he said slowly. "I knew what I was doing was wrong. I couldn't justify it like the others did. Now God is judging me and I'm going to die."

The interviewer was obviously embarrassed by his words. Interviews with AIDS victims were supposed to rouse sympathy for the homosexual community, and Jamie's painful honesty did not fit his script. But Jamie would not be silenced.

"Night after night with different people. Half the time I didn't even know their names. I knew it was wrong but I was trapped." He paused, staring bitterly at the camera. "Now look where I am." He gestured at the hospital bed, at the array of tubes entering his body, at the masked nurses.

The interviewer took over, explaining away Jamie's words.

"You can see the pain of this man's struggle with this deadly disease and the depression it induces." He was wrong, of course. Jamie had been struggling long before he caught AIDS, and with a far more common disease—guilt. I wish that I had known him. Although little could be done for his physical condition, his guilt was curable.

Pat was a modern woman, so having an abortion didn't worry her in the least. Not at first. She had accepted the idea that right and wrong were a matter of opinion. But after the abortion that began to change. Her heart began to tell her that the destruction of the new life within her had been horribly wrong, and none of her feminist logic could still that painful voice. Guilt hurt.

Guilt is a dragon that obsesses its victim. It is not easily escaped. When you run you find his fiery breath has gone ahead, hedging you in on either side, until at last your whole life is haunted by it. Pat did not run away. She faced up to her guilt and began to search for the forgiveness that destroys guilt forever. She found that only God dispenses dragon-defeating healing.

God answered Pat's long, agonized prayers one day when she stopped her car at a stoplight. She felt sure, all at once, that he *was* forgiving her, that she was free. She also knew that he wanted her to know him. That day she kept a job appointment and found herself being interviewed by Christians. The following Sunday she went to church with them and heard how God could forgive her. God replaced her burden of guilt with an infectious joy that came to mark her as she grew in her Christian life. When guilt is gone, joy takes over.

A Persistent Old Dragon
Guilt is an ancient problem that we moderns banished years ago. Right? Wrong. Like it or not, our deep-seated awareness of the

ancient laws of right and wrong resists stubbornly all attempts to declare them null and void. In fact, modern people are the most guilt ridden of all.

Perhaps you joined the "sexual revolution" and now, disillusioned, you regret the things you did, wondering if your life has been damaged beyond repair. It is even worse if you suffer physical consequences as a perpetual reminder. Or you are divorced, and deep within lies an ugly brew of bitter regrets, self-blame and rejection. Or perhaps you blame yourself for the way your child turned out.

The opportunities for guilt seem endless. These are guilt feelings that may stem from real guilt, the result of directly violating God's laws.

Some, however, are haunted by vague, unfocused guilt feelings. We are so sadly confused! Perhaps your parents divorced and, like so many children, you blamed yourself for what they did. You feel guilty, but the feelings are not founded on true guilt, true offense against the rules of life. It's irrational, and you know it, but you can't escape.

In the menagerie of dragons inhabiting our minds, there is none worse than the dragon of guilt. His deadly potency goes far beyond feelings, which is why modern therapies so often fail. Sometimes hopelessness cripples his victims, as day after day they live out a guilty lifestyle.

The first issue to be faced is the reality of objective guilt. What if I feel guilty because I *am* guilty? What is the cure?

Guilty As Charged

Peter had disowned his Lord. Christ was about to be executed. Three times with violent language Peter denied that he even knew Jesus. The guilt of that memory haunted Peter, and even seeing Jesus after the resurrection had not solved the problem.

Jesus had to deal with his guilty disciple in a more direct way. It happened early one morning as Peter and a couple of the other disciples were returning from a night's fishing. They saw a man on the shore, not recognizing him as Jesus.

He called out to them, "Friends, haven't you any fish?"

"No," they answered.

He said, "Throw your net on the right side of the boat and you will find some." When they did, they were unable to haul the net in because of the large number of fish.

Then the disciple whom Jesus loved said to Peter, "It is the Lord!" As soon as Simon Peter heard him say "It is the Lord," he wrapped his outer garment around him (for he had taken it off) and jumped into the water. The other disciples followed in the boat, towing the net full of fish, for they were not far from shore, about a hundred yards. When they landed, they saw a fire of burning coals there with fish on it, and some bread.

Jesus said to them, "Bring some of the fish you have just caught."

Simon Peter climbed aboard and dragged the net ashore. (Jn 21:5-11)

Even though Peter's guilt is not directly referred to here, it hangs as a dark backdrop to the entire encounter. It explains Peter's strained reactions.

No doubt Peter had many reasons for returning to Galilee, but one major reason was likely that he wanted to escape from Jerusalem, the scene where he had failed his friend. How natural for him to seek healing and forgetfulness in the familiar tasks of his earlier career as a fisherman! So he went fishing. He knew about fishing, the nets felt right in his hands, and the lake was blessedly familiar. To escape his guilt, he soaked himself in friendly places.

But, of course, it didn't work. Sooner or later the issue must be faced. Peter had to confront his guilt openly if he was ever to be free. Jesus knew that. Escapism, whether by returning to familiar settings or by plunging into a whirl of new experiences, is disastrous. Guilt must be faced, recognized for what it is and dealt with.

Jesus loved Peter too much to allow the evasion to continue, and so he intervened. Standing on the shore he told them to cast their net over the other side of the boat. They obeyed and had a tremendous catch. Realizing what had happened, John said to Peter, "It's the Lord."

Peter's next actions reveal a common pattern among the guilt ridden—he went overboard, literally! Everybody else was content to quietly row to the shore, but not Peter. Taking off his coat, Peter jumped into the water and flapped his way to land. He simply *had* to be with Jesus.

Then Jesus said, "Peter, we need something to eat—how about some of those fish that I arranged for you to catch?" Peter rushed over to the boat to bring the entire netful of fish to Jesus! Enthusiasm? Yes, and something more.

Have you ever been in Peter's situation? Have you run around in ever-decreasing circles, working hard to rid yourself of the feelings of guilt? We seem to think that if we can only run fast enough we will finally get away from the ache within. But it doesn't work.

I know it doesn't work because I've tried. As a teen-ager I was dared to steal a fountain pen from a local drugstore. Such pens were quite the thing in those days, and I felt very brave going in. But as I approached the counter, the tension began to build. I reached out my sweating hand to take the pen as it lay in tempting splendor on its silken bed. Then the pen was safely in my pocket. Sauntering nonchalantly toward the entrance, I found that my legs had developed a strange tendency to wobble off in wrong directions. Every step became a huge effort. Sweat poured from my body, my face grew hot, and the entrance seemed to back away from me as I approached. The watchful assistant at the door bent his piercing eyes on me. Surely he would discover me? Then I was outside. Taking to my heels, I was moments later the center of an admiring crowd of friends.

But then something strange happened. The pen changed. It now looked cheap and tawdry. And I changed. I didn't want it anymore. Wandering away from my friends, I felt the pen burning in my pocket. Every sound seemed to herald an angry storekeeper with police in attendance. I imagined the haunted life stretching ahead of me, every dream about my getting caught, every policeman seeming to be after me. I relived the agonizing moments of my escape from the store over and over. Would the storekeeper recognize me? Could I trust my friends? Of course not. And I knew the theft had not been worth the price I was beginning to pay. I dropped the hateful pen in a pond, hoping never to see it again. Guilt I was not so easily rid of.

Yet guilt and the guilt feelings that make us act strangely can be erased from our lives. But we cannot do it ourselves, any more than Peter could. Peter could only handle his guilt when he sat down quietly over breakfast and listened to what Jesus had to say.

Why This Aching Inside?

Peter was struggling with a *real* issue and so are we. Guilt feelings that stem from things we have done can only be removed when our actions themselves are dealt with. Dealing with the feelings alone never works because guilt is not just a feeling. We are guilty because we have done wrong. That wrongness is not a feeling—it's a fact.

Peter knew his guilt was real, that it was grounded in reality. He had declared to Jesus, "Even if everybody else leaves you, I will stay with you. You can trust me. I won't let you down." But within hours Peter did exactly that. After Jesus' arrest Peter followed him into the high priest's house. There, while Jesus was being interrogated in a mockery of a trial, Peter denied him— denied that he even knew him—three times. Scripture tells us that when Peter realized what he had done, he broke down, crying bitterly.

Peter's anguish was real, and the guilt behind it was just as real. He had failed God. Peter *felt* guilty because he *was* guilty.

And he had to face it. Ignoring true guilt is no solution. Society in general has announced that anything goes sexually, that there is nothing wrong in complete relations between two caring people. So why do I meet so many students struggling with a sense of guilt? Why do so many young couples who had sex before marriage have such trouble with sex after the wedding? Is it not because, in spite of our new morality, some level of our consciousness is aware of wrongdoing, of true guilt which stubbornly remains long after we have banished it? Sex beyond the sphere of marriage where God planted it has become invested with guilt and guilt feelings, all our attempts to supersede God's standards with our own notwithstanding.

What are we to do with these unwelcome feelings we have? We must trace them back to their base in true guilt. And when we face up to our guilt, we find ourselves, like Peter, face to face with God. For guilt comes when I violate his law of right and wrong. His law, like his very existence, stands independent of me and my opinion. Like it or not, I am created with his law "built in," and that is why I *know* that my guilt feelings can be trusted to tell me something true about myself and God. I am guilty before him.

The good news is that the Judge I face is one who cares for me and who is personally disappointed in my actions. I have let him down. Admitting my guilt is the beginning of the answer.

There are a couple of exceptions to the scenario as I've painted it. The first relates to those whose guilt feelings are really a reflections of others' guilt, not their own. For example, children who have been sexually abused often struggle with guilt feelings. They tell themselves that they are bad for doing such things, not fully realizing they are victims of the wrong actions of others. Such children sometimes generate a pattern of guilt feelings that continue on in later life, feelings that have no root in reality.

A second exception occurs in those who ignore the voice of conscience so long that eventually they cease to hear it. Their conscience becomes seared, burnt and scarred, "as with a hot iron." They can do the most wicked and terrible things and feel nothing. Every day people like this parade through our courts of justice, men and women who are indeed guilty before God and others but who reveal total indifference to what they have done. If you don't listen to the voice of your conscience, if you ignore it, if you try to deny the fact of guilt, you too can sear your conscience so that you can get rid of its painful voice and cease to feel anything at all. But that is no blessing. It is stark tragedy.

First Steps in Healing

Feeling guilt but going no further is destructive. Its purpose is to bring us to Jesus. Peter let guilt do its work in him. By the sunlit lakeside he came at last face to face with the One whom he had offended, the One who alone could deal with his guilt.

Jesus went straight to the violated relationship, asking, "Peter, do you love me?" He might have added, ". . . after all you've done?" but he didn't need to. Peter was feeling the overwhelming sorrow that goes with guilt.

Like a master surgeon Jesus opens the wound and releases the sorrow to produce repentance. In 2 Corinthians 7:10 we read, "Godly sorrow brings repentance that leads to salvation and leaves no regret, but worldly sorrow brings death." Peter was on his way to repentance. Grieving for what he had done, he was accepting responsibility.

Peter's sorrow was constructive, as ours must be. It enabled him to face what he had done. It will make us say, "I'm going to put those things right. I'm going to make reparation where possible, and where I've hurt people I'm going to try and help." Godly sorrow leads to repentance.

There is another kind of sorrow. It is the empty, hand-wringing kind that makes us repeat fruitlessly, "If only . . ." Instead of leading us to God, these feelings of guilt remain to torment us, leading "to death."

Sorrow that leads to repentance is conscious of its helplessness. Listen to the helplessness in Peter's response to Jesus. He wants to say, "Lord, of course I love you." But he had declared his devotion once before and failed. His love had been proved unreliable, his good intentions faithless. This sense of helplessness shapes Peter's awkward, uncomfortable replies.

When you face the Lord Jesus with your guilt, you too will need to be aware of your helplessness. Paul knew it, writing, "I do not understand what I do. For what I want to do I do not do, but what I hate I do. . . . What a wretched man I am! Who will rescue me from this body of death?" (Rom 7:15, 24). It is the cry of one who feels helpless in the face of his guilt.

Why are we helpless? First, we are helpless because there is nothing we can do to change the past. It is unreachable. Second, we are helpless because we are by nature inadequate. Peter was saying, in effect, "Lord, I love you, but I loved you before and it wasn't enough. I know what I ought to do, but in spite of loving you I don't seem to be able to do it." Yet Peter's hopelessness was key to his deliverance. *The purpose of our guilt experience is to drive us to God with our helplessness because Jesus is able to deal with it.*

When you look at your life honestly, do you find the hidden tensions of guilt? As you unpack your memories, does guilt spill from the wrappings? It comes from little things like lies and angry words. It comes from wrong decisions. It comes from childhood selfishness, from teen-age rebellion, from adult willfulness, from angry confrontations and quiet resentments—and we ache with regret as we remember them.

Don't hide these things away any longer. The time has come to take them out, face them and let the poison drain away. But it must be done with Jesus. You may have hurt many people with your actions, but most of all you have hurt God. You didn't intend it, but it is true just the same. Because he loves you, he suffers through all the things you do. The cross is a window into what that pain is like.

The first step is to face the Lord. You will find him ready to free you from the past and to forgive you utterly.

The Ultimate Answer

God is much more concerned about our guilt than we are. The difference is that he has a solution. Jesus specializes in dealing with guilt, and there really is no reason why this dragon should be haunting our lives at all. In the forgiveness won by Jesus Christ we have the decisive, complete answer for dealing with guilt once and for all. God's plan has no loose ends.

The cross is a cosmic transaction in which God raised one hand in judgment over our sinful race and the other hand in blessing over the one perfect Man—and then crossed his hands.

As Peter was later to say, "Christ died for sins once for all, the righteous for the unrighteous, to bring you to God" (1 Pet 3:18).

The Judge of all the earth has taken your guilt on his own shoulders. The suffering of the cross was his judgment against your guilt, but he bore it instead of you. You go free. In his plan God has not ignored human guilt. It has been judged and punished. When you admit your helplessness, Jesus steps in and bears your guilt away.

This superb transaction is the core of the Christian message. Guilt is gone! As Paul exults, "Therefore, there is now no condemnation. . . . Who will bring any charge against those whom God has chosen? It is God who justifies. . . . If God is for us, who can be against us?" (Rom 8:1, 33, 31). Guilt has been cut off at its root. The *fact* of guilt which underlies the feelings of guilt has been removed.

Although it was half a lifetime away, I remember clearly when I first grasped what Jesus had done for me. A pretty girl had persuaded me to go with her to a tiny country church she attended. I went because it was the only place she would go on a Sunday night. That night it was as if the preacher were preaching just for me, and during the last hymn (which seemed to have a hundred verses) I found myself gripped with a longing to be free from my past. It wasn't a long past, but it was ugly and its guilt was weighing me down.

I ended up alone at the front, feeling dreadfully embarrassed but very determined to be rid of my burden. When the preacher prayed with me, I simply knew beyond doubt that my guilt before God had gone, all of it. I was free—not just from the guilt but from the life-sapping feelings of guilt.

I also remember the first time I shared the story of forgiveness with a friend. I literally saw his guilt falling away in a moment as his face turned from pain to joy. It was like watching the sun come out.

It has always been that way. Augustine experienced it seventeen centuries ago. His guilt had brought him to an apparent dead end as he sat weeping in a garden. Then he heard a child's voice from a nearby house singing, "Take and read, take and read." Opening the Bible, he read the words which changed his life. He described it like this: "No further would I read; nor needed I: for instantly at the end of this sentence, by a light as it were of serenity infused into my heart, all the darkness of doubt vanished away."[1] A thousand years later the monk Martin Luther found the same sweet sense of God's forgiveness and cried out, "For me it was, for me he died!"

Great or small, ancient or modern, we all need forgiveness. This is the road to peace and freedom from guilt. To know it, you too must add your name to the list of the freed—Peter, Paul, Augustine, Luther and *you*. God cannot and will not force the release on you. You have to want it and choose it for yourself. Isn't it amazing, after all God has done to set us free from the painful burden of guilt, that it should come down to this? But that is the way God has chosen—to lay his magnificent offer out and then wait for our response.

This is where faith comes in. At the shore of the Sea of Tiberius, in the cold freshness of early morning, Peter faced this great decision. Jesus was ready to reinstate him as a leader of his flock. He repeated the words Peter had first heard three years before: "Follow me."

It meant that Jesus was willing and able to forgive, to treat Peter as though his denials had never been. But Peter must first make his choice. He had to abandon his regrets and his defeats and throw himself helplessly onto Jesus' love. And so must we, for there is no other way to be free.

Look deep into the eyes of Jesus, and let him see your guilt. Love him, trust him, and *let your guilt go*.

But I Have Been Too Bad

I have lost count of the people who have missed God's forgiveness because of the lie that they have been too bad. People tell me that I wouldn't talk so readily of forgiveness if I knew what they had done. My answer is always the same: "Tell me." When the painful recital of the past is over and the sin is out in the open between us, we take a clear look at it. For some it has been marital unfaithfulness; for some, theft; for some, incest or violence. We have many ways of damaging ourselves and others. But by God's truth I can look at them all unafraid and declare firmly that the cross of Jesus covers them all.

Do you believe that? Or are you still thinking that you can exhaust God's ability to forgive? Think what that means for a moment. The death of God's own Son, sent specifically from heaven for this, is insufficient? I have to say as gently as I can that you are mistaken. Jesus has never, and will never, face any sin that he cannot deal with through his cross. The only unforgivable sin is to deny him the opportunity, that is, to reject his offer of himself (Mk 3:29).

Perhaps you have been a Christian and have wandered from him, and you are saying, "There is no forgiveness for me." Perhaps God's forgiveness is rationed and you have used up your quota? Not so. Come back to him. The cross covers this too. No matter what you have done, no matter where you have wandered, no matter how often you have fallen, his arms reach out to embrace and forgive. Let it go.

Guilt Feelings: The Dragon's Last Fling

Once Jesus has removed our guilt, we can deal with our feelings of guilt. Sometimes they vanish immediately with the experience of forgiveness. Sometimes they linger, as if unaware that they have no base. Sometimes they appear to have gone but recur unannounced.

Don't be surprised if you experience guilt feelings now and then. You are still able to remember what you have done in the past. The enemy's aim is to raise these memories *just as though you had never been forgiven.* He wants you to think that you really have not been forgiven. He wants you to go on condemning yourself for things God has already dealt with.

This is a lie which needs to be handled like other lies, by asserting strongly the facts of faith.

Resolutely take those thoughts as they come and nail them to the cross. Insist that the feeling no longer corresponds with reality and repeat—aloud if necessary—"God has justified me, Jesus has died for me, it is over." Then deliberately praise him for your new sense of forgiveness.

Guilt feelings fade steadily under such an assault of faith. If you insist on cutting off each head of the dragon of guilt as it appears, in time even that multiheaded monster will flee from you. When the truth makes you free, you are free indeed.

Questions for Individuals or Groups

1. How do those who do not know the Bible know right from wrong?

2. How can a conscience become conditioned to experience false guilt?

Have you experienced this? How can we be set free?

3. This chapter described how some modern psychologies banish guilt by making morals a matter of opinion. Why doesn't this work in practice?

4. Read John 21:5-11. Why didn't Jesus refer to Peter's guilt problem?

How exactly does Jesus heal Peter's guilt?

5. How would you deal with someone who felt their sins were too bad to be forgiven?

6. Why didn't God declare us to be forgiven without the cross?

7. How would you help someone who has believed in the cross and yet still has difficulty feeling forgiven?

2
Overcoming Anger

Controlling the
Fire Inside

When we have had a bout with one dragon and experienced the joy of its defeat, we are tempted to lay down our weapons for a short rest. But we dare not rest long.

In fact, with eyes closed, turned inward to view the landscape of the mind, we might see enough dragon prints to give us a good scare. Just ahead, looming beyond the Plain of Comfortable Behavior, lies the threatening peak of Mounting Anger. It is a basic part of our nature, an important part of our mind's terrain, but we are uneasily aware that it can be a mountain lair for all kinds of dragons—bitterness, sarcasm, cruelty, violence and all their ugly brood.

Things are generally predictable at the local McDonald's restaurant. It's a good, safe place to take the kids—usually. But when anger took control of one man outside a San Diego McDonald's, over twenty people were murdered. James Huberty stepped inside with an automatic gun in each hand and killed every man, woman and child who entered until a police marksman felled him. Why? "He was always angry," his wife and neighbors said. Perhaps it began in his childhood when his mother left him. Anger grew, festering over the years, fed by every slight or misfortune until at last it exploded in fury. Anger needs careful handling!

Almost everyone is angry at one time or another. We can all recall the aftermath of pounding heart, clenched jaw, tense muscles and a strong sense of discomfort. We don't like anger and it unsettles us when others get angry. We walk quickly away, embarrassed.

Some of us are angry most of the time. In too many homes angry parents let their rage explode on the vulnerable, their children. Child abuse has become horrifyingly widespread in our society. Beaten wives, murders, rapes—the evidence of anger let loose is all around us. No wonder our own anger frightens us!

Sometimes anger is buried beneath passive behavior. But anger begets anger, and abused people often store their anger away until later, when it erupts on unsuspecting people. That is why the beaten child so often becomes a child beater. When we experience the release of anger long stored from our past, exploding from deep inside with a force we never suspected, we are surprised and horrified.

Why We Get Angry
I was once caught in a traffic jam on a section of freeway. It was at a time in my life when I felt I had made some progress in my Christian life. I had been trying to grow out of impatience and irritability and was congratulating myself on becoming more serene and controlled. On this particular day I had been tied up in a research meeting at the university where I taught. It had run

late. I was due to leave for another meeting where I was to speak that evening, and I was not even home yet. I would no doubt have to miss dinner. Meanwhile, here I was, stuck in almost stationary traffic on a hot, sticky, midwestern summer day. The car ahead moved ten yards forward to open a space for me to move into.

Just then a big, ugly black Cadillac, driven by an equally ugly, overbearing man, smoking an ugly, fat cigar, swept up the hard shoulder alongside the line of cars and swerved into my vacant space.

My hard-won serenity exploded, my newfound patience expired, and my anger took over. For the next two miles I kept my front bumper within an inch of his. Worse still, my finger pressed the horn button for minutes on end and, worst of all, I found myself shouting out the window at this severe abuse of my civil rights!

Of course, professors think they can get away with that kind of thing, but now that I am a pastor it is a different story! Now I have the feeling that everyone I have ever preached to is sitting in the car right behind me at such moments. Their invisible presence certainly motivates me to choose control, but even with the help of that watching congregation, it is not easy to rein in anger. To slay this dragon we need first to understand it.

The wise book of Proverbs isolates four causes for anger, all of which I experienced that day: injustice, humiliation, imitation and frustration.

The first two, *injustice and humiliation,* together tap into a deep human need for significance. Relating to injustice, the proverb says, "A harsh word stirs up anger" (Prov 15:1). Any time our rights or even our imagined rights are violated, we are in danger of a selfish explosion of retaliation.

The writer of the proverbs knew of the humiliation that slander stirs up: "A gossip separates close friends" (Prov 16:28). We sense the injustice when we find people gossiping about us. And the humiliation leads quickly to anger. *Anger is our explosive response to a denial of our significance.*

Suppose you are standing in line to buy a hamburger, patiently waiting your turn. Into the store walks a self-important man, the kind of person who knows that the entire universe exists for his convenience alone. In his loud polyester suit he walks to the front of your line and aggressively announces his order. How do you feel? Angry? Yes, indeed. And why? He treated you as if you weren't there, as if you didn't count. That is what infuriates us so, what arouses our sense of injustice.

When we feel we have not been treated fairly, our anger is saying, "You *will* pay attention to me! I *do* matter!" We are fighting a threat to our sense of worth. Since our sense of self-worth is our internal definition of who we are, these attacks are the psychological equivalent of a threat to our lives, and our anger generates the pounding heart and clenched fists appropriate to physical self-defense.

This understanding gives a clue to how we can change for the better. Angry people are insecure and therefore easily threatened. Our cure is a deeper sense of security in who we are and in our significance as people.

The third source of anger named in Proverbs is *imitation:* "Do not make friends with a hot-tempered man, do not associate with one easily angered, or you may learn his ways and get yourself ensnared" (Prov 22:24). Anger is infectious. It only takes one angry member of a household for the "disease" to spread among the rest. Anger becomes our defense against the unjust aggression we meet in each contact with an angry friend or family member.

Within marriage an irritable partner will generate resentment (another form of anger) in his or her spouse. It is not always obvious. For example, an aggressive, bullying husband may seem to have reduced his wife to a doormat. She never responds to his attacks for fear of abuse. Watch them carefully, however, and you will see that she has developed subtle ways of goading him, just short of setting off his violence. Her beaten-down air may be part of this. Her behavior says, in effect, "This is what you get for being nasty to me!" The dirty house, the sexual unresponsiveness, the little comments that undermine him—it is an underground (often unconscious) warfare. She has learned to twist the lion's tail, but it is a dangerous business. Couples like this live in perpetual anger with each other, and their children suffer the consequences.

Frustration is the fourth cause of anger we find in Scripture. "Starting a quarrel is like breaching a dam" (Prov 17:14). Anger can build up a pressure which in time vents off in an explosion. A sequence of irritating events during the day can build up pressure until finally a relatively insignificant event can trigger off an eruption. Often children are the unwitting last straw, setting off an already angry parent.

Other times the anger is stored up for years. You may be angry with your mother and transfer it all to your longsuffering wife. You may be angry at all your father did to you as a child, and now your husband or boyfriend breaks the dam your father built and gets the total flood dumped on him.

Take a moment to evaluate yourself. Look back on your recent reactions. Are you angry or irritable? Have you stored up the anger-pressure from the past? Perhaps it comes from your childhood. Perhaps it is a later experience of rejection that wounded you deeply. Is it poisoning your reaction to other people in your life now? Do you burn with a short fuse so that others tiptoe around you for fear of setting you off?

Cliff had had a terrible day. It began with a car that wouldn't start, making him late for work—on the one day the boss was early. He sprinted up the office stairs, arriving hot and sweaty before his irate boss, who demanded to know where he had been and then refused to wait for an answer. That was only the beginning. The computer broke down, a major delivery failed to arrive, and fourteen angry customers rejected his apologetic explanations. Each time he reminded himself of the company motto, "The customer is always right," and each time the customer was not only wrong but abusive. Cliff struggled home, desperate for sanctuary from a cruel world, seething inwardly at the injustice of life.

When he opened the door, Cliff tripped over the dog lying inconsiderately inside the doorway and fell into the room. His teen-age son was, as usual, playing a rock record at full blast, and his daughter was sitting zombie-like in front of the television painting her toenails. That was it. Cliff's fuse blew at last at a world that seemed to be determined to goad him. For ten minutes he became a human volcano. His indignation poured over his nearest and dearest, from wife down to dog. Soon he felt better. No longer angry at the boss and the customers, Cliff was able to sit down in peace. But his alienated son was in his room in a mutinous silence while his daughter cried up a storm of resentful tears. His wife had retired to the kitchen, her plans for a family dinner in ruins, her lips firmly zipped in disappointment.

People are remarkably resilient, and if Cliff's normal family life is warm and healthy they will all probably recover without much damage. But suppose it happened every day. Soon mother will warn the children, "Watch out now. Your father is due home." Each will retire to a private corner and tiptoe around, fearful of setting off the volcano. A long, resentful silence will replace what there once was of family conversation and laughter.

Anger let loose to serve our selfishness is nasty indeed.

Anger, however, is not always wrong. In spite of its repugnance to us, there are times when anger is appropriate. Anger can be the right response in some situations. God's anger is always right. But anger in the hands of fallen creatures like us is dangerous.

What we need is a guide to the truth about anger, an understanding of self-control and a plan to apply the healing balm of forgiveness. These are major biblical themes, so we turn to the wisdom of God's Word for some practical answers.

When Anger Is Good

God is not afraid to be angry, and the phrase "the wrath of God" comes up frequently in Scripture. His wrath is the reaction of a holy and righteous God against sin, which is a violation of the good world he has made. In particular, God's wrath is associated with the day of judgment, when his standards and the justice of his judgment will be revealed for all to see (Rom 2:5).

Jesus Christ is the complete revelation of God's perfect ways, and he was sometimes angry. Let's look at two occasions where his anger was roused, especially noting the cause of his sharp reaction.

In the first scene we find him in the synagogue. It is the Sabbath. In front of Jesus is a man with a shriveled hand, and standing around are enemies waiting to pounce if Jesus heals on the Sabbath. "He looked around at them in anger and, deeply distressed at their stubborn hearts, said to the man, 'Stretch out your hand' " (Mk 3:5). And he healed the man's hand. God's wrath in Romans 2:5 and Jesus' anger in Mark 3:5 are both aroused by human stubbornness. Jesus was angry because his pious opponents cared nothing for the man's suffering and only saw him as an opportunity to attack Jesus. This hard, vindictive stubbornness blinded them to truth and goodness, and that is what made Jesus angry—not just angry at them but also angry for them.

The same thing appears even more clearly when Jesus turns on the Pharisees during that last week before he was crucified. In some of the most biting prose in the Gospels he lashes out at them: "Woe to you, teachers of the law and Pharisees, you hypocrites! You shut the kingdom of heaven in men's faces. You yourselves do not enter, nor will you let those enter who are trying to. Woe to you, teachers of the law and Pharisees, you hypocrites! You travel over land and sea to win a single convert, and when he becomes one, you make him twice as much a son of hell as you are" (Mt 23:13-15).

Jesus' anger here is in defense of those who have been trapped and misled by the Pharisees' and lawyers' teaching. His anger burns on behalf of others.

There is more here than just that, however. Jesus has already used reason and gentleness during his ministry, but these stubborn men have rejected both. Here we see his last urgent effort to get through to them, to convince them of the danger of what they are doing to themselves. Anger is his last resort, a verbal hammer blow to break the hardened shell they have developed against God's appeal to their hearts.

The anger of Jesus, then, was unselfish, arising out of his concern for both the abused and the abuser. It reflected his commitment to righteousness.

So we cannot simply dismiss anger as though it were always inappropriate or wrong. Nevertheless, our fears of anger are well founded. The ageless wisdom of the Bible notes that "a quick-tempered man displays folly" (Prov 14:29). There is no doubt that we are far more likely to make fools of ourselves when we are angry than at any other time. The reason is that anger is a powerful emotion, and when we are in its grip we act instinctively rather than by reason or forethought. Usually our rage will expose, magnified, our own worst traits, whether selfishness, self-righteousness or sheer inability to control the tongue.

Because of these things, anger is frowned on in many circles as uncivilized and inappropriate. This is especially true among Christians. The Bible gives no support to such an idea. On the contrary, we might be more effective in changing our society if we allowed anger its godly place in our lives.

There is an urgent need for righteous anger. One organization working with runaways has estimated that within a few blocks of Times Square in New York several thousand teen-agers of both sexes between the ages of twelve and seventeen are enslaved in vice rings. Now that should make us angry!

A daily scientific slaughter produces in our country a million and a half abortions yearly. That should make us angry!

Routine trafficking in hard drugs is hardening and destroying many of our youth while it enriches the leaders of organized crime. That should make us angry! And so should the inadequacy of our society's response.

People are starving in a world which could provide for them. The obscenity of child pornography, brutality to women and children, the death toll from drunken drivers—all these things should fuel a steady anger.

Anger is part of God's design to move his people out of apathy and into action. As long as we are frightened of our anger, just so long will our response to evil be ineffective. What we need is not less anger, but more of it—properly directed.

Like Jesus' anger, our anger must be directed in support of the helpless and the downtrodden, instead of in our own defense. Like Jesus' anger, ours must be part of an unselfish lifestyle. The great question is then, how do I learn to control this emotion and channel it to appropriate uses?

Developing Self-Control

Self-control in Scripture is not a human discipline. It is part of the fruit of the Spirit. It is the supernatural result of the Holy Spirit living in the believing heart. Here then is the solution to lives dominated by bitterness and anger. You need help beyond yourself to control such things when they are endemic in your life, and Jesus offers just this help. Resolve to take him as your Lord and follow in his ways. As you do so, he promises that his spirit will indwell you, enabling you to develop the self-control you need.

Self-control does not just arrive full-blown, however. God never sets aside human freedom in that way, for he created us to be free. The New Testament never regards Christians as mindless, programmed robots, but as responsible people who are now expected to behave with integrity and backbone.

An analogy may help to explain how the Spirit's power interacts with human will. A modern jet is controlled by pilots who steer the plane by the half-wheel steering columns. How do they manage to move those huge wing flaps with their meager human strength? Not by their strength at all. The pilot simply adjusts the steering column according to which way he or she wants the plane to move. A powerful hydraulic system backs up his puny force and actually moves the flaps.

In the same way, God's Spirit within you provides ample power to live obediently. But you still have to choose to fight temptation rather than giving in. Paul tells us how to do that. "You were taught, with regard to your former way of life, to put off your old self, which is being corrupted by its deceitful desires; to be made new in the attitude of your minds; and to put on the

new self, created to be like God in true righteousness and holiness" (Eph 4:22-24).

This process of putting off the old self with its ways and
putting on the new can only be accomplished in the power of
the Holy Spirit, who formed this new self when he entered our
lives. But the choice to live out the new life requires continual
decision making on our part. So Paul continues, " 'In your anger
do not sin': Do not let the sun go down while you are still angry,
and do not give the devil a foothold" (Eph 4:26-27).

Retraining Your Brain

Think of your brain as a soft, sandy surface, with your thoughts
like water flowing across it. At first the water flows anywhere on
the surface, but soon it creates channels and then the water flows
only in the channels. At first your thoughts and your behavior
can go anywhere, but soon you develop habits, *channels on the
surface of your mind*, as you repeat your thoughts and actions
again and again. As the pattern deepens, you no longer think out
your path consciously. Your thoughts just naturally flow down
your habit channel.

Now if you have developed a pattern of angry thoughts and
behavior, your mind is deeply grooved. It will take conscious
effort to change and to generate new channels.

Did you ever make a habit of crunching the gears on your car
by letting the clutch pedal up before you had finished changing
gear? It's hard to stop because it's a habit, a groove in the mind.
You don't think about changing gear. You just do it. To get rid
of the habit, you take conscious control of your thought life.
"Foot down. Change gear. Release the clutch slowly." Over and
over you do it until you develop a new, correct thought channel.
You have retrained your brain.

There are three steps to take to retrain your brain's anger

responses. First, refuse to let your thoughts go down the usual path. Of course, your immediate response is simply, "It can't be done!" But it can, and you have done it yourself. Surely you have sometime been a part of an angry, shouting scene when the phone rang. Your voice instantly switched from the volcanic to a gentle politeness, saying, "Yes, who is it?" You *can* control yourself!

The next time you feel an angry scene developing, determine to simply walk away. Don't explain; just excuse yourself and walk away. If you are in an angry marriage, try to agree beforehand to this approach. Agree together that walking away from a scene is a victory for you both, not another act of rejection. Then do it. Proverbs 14:29 reminds us, "A patient man has great understanding, but a quick-tempered man displays folly."

The second step is to pray, especially for your antagonist. Try to see how God is seeking to use the situation to help that person grow, and ask yourself how you can be part of the process.

The final and most difficult part of retraining the brain is to perform the new action. Deliberately and consciously behave graciously. Do it over and over again until at last you start to do it naturally. Eventually your thoughts and actions will flow in the new grooves. Paul in Romans quotes from the book of Proverbs to tell us how we are to treat our antagonist: " 'If your enemy is hungry, feed him; if he is thirsty, give him something to drink. In doing this, you will heap burning coals on his head.' Do not be overcome by evil, but overcome evil with good." (Rom 12:20-21)

Paul is describing the new lifestyle that Christians are to practice with the Spirit's aid. The key to growth in this area is consistency. You cannot live selfishly and self-indulgently most of the time and expect self-control when anger suddenly threatens. Paul is advocating a day-by-day policy of unselfishness, acting for the interests of others. Continued choosing of unselfish actions builds self-control so that, when anger comes, self-control is instinctive.

> Do not let any unwholesome talk come out of your mouths, but only what is helpful for building others up according to their needs, that it may benefit those who listen. And do not grieve the Holy Spirit of God, with whom you were sealed for the day of redemption. Get rid of all bitterness, rage and anger, brawling and slander, along with every form of malice. Be kind and compassionate to one another, forgiving each other, just as in Christ God forgave you. (Eph 4:29-32)

There is no room in the Christian life for bitterness, malice or anger. Let them go! Every day practice compassion and understanding as a lifestyle, and self-control will steadily become characteristic. The Holy Spirit is at work to develop these traits in our life, and our efforts are in cooperation with his empowering.

Three attitudes on our part will particularly encourage the process of change. We can develop a sense of perspective, a sense of dignity and a sense of humor.

We need a new perspective. Daily Bible study is important because it develops a heaven-oriented view of things. As we cultivate a biblical understanding of people, we come to see why they are frustrated and prone to anger. Many are lost and troubled. Because they have no relationship with God, they cannot make sense out of their lives. From heaven's perspective our appropriate response is compassion. We should no more take their anger personally than we do the anger of a frustrated child. Personal insults and violated rights are to be expected from the world which crucified our Lord. They are a reflection of the wrongness of this world. By keeping in the Word, we will lower our expectations of other people and be built up with God's love for even the unlovely.

We can develop a sense of dignity. C. S. Lewis wrote once that all people are on their way to becoming either creatures so loathsome that we meet them now only in nightmares, or creatures so glorious that we would be strongly inclined to worship them if we could see them as they will be. This high view of human destiny lends unique distinction to our present condition. If someone pushes into the line in front of us, surely we can afford to be generous when we remember that we are destined to be glorious. Let them have the hamburgers first! Are you an aggressive driver? Then remember who you really are. Creatures destined to shine like stars in eternity are much too important to get agitated over a dented fender. As we cultivate a high view of ourselves as children of God, destined for Christlikeness in eternity, much that infuriates us now will pale into insignificance.

Finally, *we can develop a sense of humor.* Humor is key to the joy that the Bible insists is to be a staple of Christian experience. Christian, laugh a lot! Practice joy on a daily basis. The confrontations that lead to anger are often hilarious when viewed rightly. Here is a place to apply the eternal perspective you are gaining from your Bible reading. We often argue fiercely over the most trivial things. Step back next time, reflect on what really matters, and give a better response than harsh words. A deep chuckle might do nicely.

What to Do in the Heat of Rage

The techniques we have considered so far are helpful in developing a self-controlled lifestyle, but they do not go to the root of anger. The Bible insists that we must seek a right internal attitude as well as being externally at peace with people. The latter without the former eventually leads to bitterness. Psychology and Scripture agree: *Repression is no solution* (Heb 12:14-15). A determination never to get angry simply causes us to internalize the problem. So instead of a blustering red face, we get stomach ulcers! Outwardly I show a sweet smile. Inwardly I seethe.

Buried anger simply re-emerges in other forms like depression, gossip, resentment, sarcasm or self-hate. If these are common in your life, look for suppressed anger as a possible cause. Look carefully at your brand of humor. Much humor is sour and bitter, as, for example, the gibes against women in many masculine jokes. Sarcasm often indicates a similar underlying anger. Unfortunately, suppressed anger is not uncommon in tightly regulated religious circles. It explains why some preachers are more inclined to attack their flock than to comfort and encourage.

While suppressing anger is no answer, neither is its opposite. The idea that every emotion must be expressed to release it leads to the self-indulgence of "encounter groups" and "primal screaming." Such things may offer the pleasant sense of emotional release, but they bring no lasting solution. They merely pander to our selfishness. Proverbs 29:11 offers this assessment: "A fool gives full vent to his anger, but a wise man keeps himself under control."

How then are we to respond in the moment of anger? We are to keep ourselves under control. But in the midst of the control, we must deal with the real problem at hand, not run from it. *Only by dealing constructively with the root cause can we find a long-term solution to anger.*

The first step toward getting at the root is to *analyze the situation* by asking the question "What is my responsibility?" If the person who has made me angry is in my life for only a moment and then gone forever, a simple strategy of self-control will do; the moment will pass. But when we live or work with a person who continually makes us angry, we have an ongoing problem that needs to be dealt with. We must begin by taking honest responsibility for our side of the problem. Perhaps we are easily irritated because of a too-busy schedule, or perhaps we have some irritating manner that arouses hostile behavior in others—and then we become angry in return. Many of us need help in our self-analysis, and counselors or friends can be invaluable.

The second step is to determine to *forego vengeance.* If, after analysis, we still find that we have been treated unfairly, we must deliberately reject any thought of hitting back. The Bible is insistent on this: "Do not repay anyone evil for evil. Be careful to do what is right is the eyes of everybody. If it is possible, as far as it depends on you, live at peace with everyone" (Rom 12:17-18). Here Paul assumes that we have completed the analysis of step one above ("as far as it depends on you") and insists on nonretaliation. He continues, "Do not take revenge, my friends, but leave room for God's wrath, for it is written: 'It is mine to avenge; I will repay,' says the Lord. On the contrary: 'If your enemy is hungry, feed him; if he is thirsty, give him something to drink. In doing this, you will heap burning coals on his head.' Do not be overcome by evil, but overcome evil with good" (Rom 12:19-21).

You cannot cure anger as long as you hold on to thoughts of retaliation. Sit down and unlock your heart before God. Pour out the poison of your resentment and bitterness before him, and *leave it there.*

Third, *plan a constructive confrontation.* If you are partly responsible, begin with an apology. Your humility will signal that you are not intending to start another round in the conflict, but that you truly desire to heal the breach. Since your antagonist will probably be expecting retaliation, work out some alternative way of signaling friendliness if an apology is not in order. A soft approach may disarm your "enemy" and open the way for reconciliation. Determine to be loving at all costs. If you are still rejected, try again later. Be patient. Deep-rooted patterns of antagonism will not vanish overnight. If, after all your efforts, you are still rejected, you have nevertheless gained something. Your sense of integrity in having sought the good of your opponent brings its own peace.

If, on the other hand, your antagonist responds to your constructive approach, be honest but tactful. Try to help him (or her) see himself clearly; but be gentle, as the process is often painful. Offer your own promise of intended changed behavior, and indicate clearly what new way of behaving on his part would avoid the problem in the future. Confrontation done this way expresses real love, the determination to pursue what is best for the other person and for the relationship between you.

The fourth step is *forgiveness*. We have already seen Paul's admonition to forgive in Ephesians 4:32. Actually, forgiveness has already begun when we forgo vengeance and plan a loving confrontation. But full forgiveness carries one more implication. It presupposes the willingness of the other person to be forgiven. Our aim must be to confront in love so that forgiveness can happen. This is what God has done for us. The Bible insists that we forgive as God does, as much as the other person will allow.

But what do we do when after confrontation in love the other person is unwilling to work toward a solution? The answer is to be at peace. There is nothing more we can do. We can be at peace because we have fully dealt with our side of the problem. At this stage the anger has gone.

When anger is disarmed and reconciliation restored, the dragon is dead. With it go its hideous offspring, and the Christian is free again to live in the fruit of the Spirit, especially love and peace. The passion that wished to trap us in self-protection can be turned outward to its proper object, to a strongly felt care for those abused by evil in our world.

Questions for Individuals or Groups

1. In what situations do you usually become angry?

Do these fit with the chapter's definition of anger as a response to a "denial of our significance"?

2. Imagine a scale starting at "peaceful," progressing through "irritated" and "frustrated" to "angry." Where are you on this scale most of the time?

Do others see you that way?

3. Reflect on the anger level in the home where you grew up. How has this affected you?

4. What are the things we *should* be angry about in our society? What are you doing about them?

5. What are the characteristics of righteous anger?

6. What is the role of the Holy Spirit and what is your role in developing self-control? (Be specific and practical.)

7. How would you advise a married couple who regularly fight to overcome their anger (a) in the short term and (b) in the long term?

8. Read Ephesians 4:29-32. Would you say your fellowship group is characterized by positive or negative speech? (If it's negative, how can you change it?)

9. How can a timid person develop the ability to confront unfairness?

3

Overcoming
Legalism

Accepting
God's Love

No one wants the beast of anger around. It is blatantly ugly as it rears its head and spumes scorching flames. We don't want to feel that dragon within us or to meet it in someone else. But the Dragon of Legalism takes us a bit off guard. This beast can look most proper and act so well behaved. Has it been the object of some unfair press?

The Dragon of Legalism reached full-blown stature years ago among the Pharisees of Jesus' time, but it has since then found a haven in Christian churches. It lurks comfortably around pulpits and assumes charge in certain strict religious homes. Is it as harmless as it appears, smiling from the corner there? Beware of this dragon! It has done more damage among God's people than almost any other dragon. The Dragon of Legalism is deadly.

A Tale Once Told

The farmer was weary as he trod his lonely way home through the fields. Aching bones took away any pleasure he may have felt in the loveliness of his valley, with the setting sun coating trees, house and fields in gold. Even the welcoming lights of home could not remove the bitter frown lines of premature age from his face.

But the farmhouse was different. As he came through the last field, he could see the bustle of unusual activity, and through the quiet evening air he could catch the sounds of music and dancing. He stopped still on the track and waited as his servant approached.

"It's your brother! He's home again and your father has ordered a celebration." Nothing could keep the excitement from the servant's voice.

The farmer slammed the flat of his hand sharply against the gate and dropped his scythe to the ground. His cheeks flushed in anger. Pointing in the direction of the house, he shouted, "He dared to come back after all he's done?"

His father lifted his head at the voice, and for a moment his smile of delight faded to weariness. But only for a moment. He moved quickly down the track, as quickly as he had moved down it so recently to welcome his younger son home. Old as he was, he moved with the eagerness of youth, and his voice was warm and rich.

"Son, you're home! What a day this is for us—your brother is back! He's learned his lesson, his attitude has changed, and all is well again. Come and join the celebration!" He reached out his arm gently to his older son's shoulder. The farmer shrugged it off, his face twisted in cold anger.

"No," he said, and, "No," again.

"Son, Son, come in, please. Don't spoil this day."

"He took half the farm," raged the older son, "and he plunged us into debt. He took the money and gave it to whores. And you give him a party! You were soft with him from the start, but when did you ever celebrate for me? I have worked for you like a slave—for nothing! I will not go in."

The father had heard the bitter refrain before. And, as before, he yearned to embrace his son, saying, "All I have is yours now, but I *have* to celebrate for my son who is home from the dead."

As Jesus came to the close of the story, the crowd sat riveted in attention. The Master Storyteller's voice had taken on the rich, loving tone of the openhearted father in his story. Two Pharisees also listened with rigid attention, exchanging looks of mutual anger. They knew who Jesus meant by the older brother.

Jesus versus the Pharisees

The contrast between a generous father and an unforgiving son was paralleled in the contrast between Jesus and the rigid Pharisees. The parable of the prodigal and his brother was designed to expose the coldness of the Pharisees' religion. It was part of that long confrontation that the Gospels describe between Jesus' teaching of free forgiveness and the Pharisees' insistence on law and punishment. In parable after parable Jesus drove the contrast home.

The Pharisees' religion was built on the strict application of the law of Moses. A Pharisee's whole life was aimed at achieving righteousness before God by keeping every detail in the 613 precepts of the law. To be extra safe, he took on himself special obligations of ritual purity that the law required only of the priests.

Pharisees interpreted the law conservatively. If there was any chance at all of infringing on the law, they would avoid the situation entirely. They called this "building a hedge around the law." They could never eat as a guest of someone not a Pharisee, for example, because the food might not be ritually pure. Nor could they buy food from non-Pharisees. It might not have been strictly tithed.

Lay people admired the rigor of Pharisaic commitment and discipline, and the Pharisees welcomed the admiration. Why not? They had earned it.

They had *earned* it. That was the flaw. They felt that they had achieved righteousness themselves. If they had, then it was reasonable to despise the traitorous tax collectors. After all, they too could have kept the law but chose not to. Self-righteousness is the inevitable pose of legalistic religionists. Jesus hated it.

The gospel story records the conflict between these two opposing views of religion. Jesus saw true religion as the joyful acceptance of God's mercy. The Pharisees saw it as a rigid adherence to the Mosaic law and tradition. Believing that they had succeeded in attaining righteousness where others had failed, they arrogantly saw themselves as a class apart from the herd. Jesus saw their attitude epitomized in the image of two men praying in the Temple, one a Pharisee and the other a repentant tax collector.

The Pharisee stands to pray. Pious hands upheld, he mouths gracious words with perfect diction, obviously speaking to a god who mirrors his own approving estimate of himself. "I thank you for the excellence of myself, so different from others—like this wretched tax collector, rejected from Israel, groveling on the floor here."

But the tax collector was not listening to him. Prostrate in repentance before the Father, he was coming home. Jesus declared him accepted of God.

And the Pharisees ground their teeth again.

Jesus saw their "success" as failure and their attitude as sinful.

He denied their claim to have successfully kept the law. Instead, he said, they had reduced the towering principles of God's law to a set of do's and don'ts. What they had kept was a pale shadow. The law itself remained beyond their actions and its spirit lay beyond their understanding.

"Woe to you, teachers of the law and Pharisees, you hypocrites! You give a tenth of your spices—mint, dill and cummin. But you have neglected the more important matters of the law—justice, mercy and faithfulness. . . . You blind guides! You strain out a gnat but swallow a camel" (Mt 23:23-24). Jesus knew the self- indulgence that hid beneath their outward piety.

"Woe to you, teachers of the law and Pharisees, you hypocrites! You clean the outside of the cup and dish, but inside they are full of greed and self-indulgence. Blind Pharisee! First clean the inside of the cup and dish, and then the outside also will be clean" (Mt 23:25-26). Jesus was forcing the issue. The Pharisees could not stand to have him expose their nakedness, their pride and dressed-up evil. They could either repent of their error, just as the tax collector had, and follow Jesus, or they would have to eliminate Jesus. There could be no compromise.

But the Pharisees in general had no intention of coming to Jesus. And Jesus knew that: "You snakes! You brood of vipers! How will you escape being condemned to hell? Therefore I am sending you prophets and wise men and teachers. Some of them you will kill and crucify; others you will flog in your synagogues and pursue from town to town" (Mt 23:33-34). So they arranged for Jesus to be killed.

For us the very name *Pharisee* has become synonymous with hypocrisy. We certainly know that the Pharisaic brand of self-righteousness is abhorrent to God. A Sunday-school teacher once told his children the story of the two men in the Temple praying. "The Pharisee looked with contempt at the tax collector on his face before God and praised God he wasn't like this miserable, sinful tax collector." Then the teacher added, "Now, children, let us pray and thank God that we are not like the Pharisee!"

It is easy to condemn legalism in others. It is hard even to detect it in ourselves. Few Pharisees, ancient or modern, ever recognize their own legalism. The awful thing about Jesus' stern attacks is that they might be directed at me.

When I was young my church youth group used to make regular forays into the inner city for evangelism. One time a friend, Jack, found himself in the rescue mission sitting by a very dirty old man. As he sat listening to the singing, tears began to run down the old man's cheeks, tracing clear lines in the dirt. My friend wanted to put his arm around the old man, but as he looked he saw something move in the old man's hair. Overcoming his revulsion, Jack did reach his arm around the limp shoulders.

I wonder if I would have done so. I think of the times I smelled the beer on a drunk lying in the alleyway—and passed by on the other side, thankful that I didn't drink. It's easy to be smug and self-approving, but we must all recognize the dragon for what it is.

In place of the Pharisees' self-righteousness, Jesus offered forgiveness. The forgiving father who welcomed home his wandering son in Jesus' story was his picture of God the Father. The elder brother talked the language of legalism. "How can you take him back after all he has done? He has earned rejection, so reject him."

But the father talks the language of love and family. "My son has come home; let's celebrate."

Over and over again Jesus demonstrated this forgiving acceptance of sinful men and women. Whether it was a sick person (assumed by the Pharisees to be sick because of sinfulness), or a traitor collecting taxes for the Romans, or a weeping prostitute, his response was the same: a warm acceptance and the call to go and sin no more. Paul explains how Jesus could be so forgiving to those who repented. He had made the way to God open through his death on the cross. "God made him who had no sin to be sin for us, so that in him we might become the righteousness of God" (2 Cor 5:21).

That was how God was to be reconciled to humans. By his own act God took our weight of sin on himself and wrapped us in the shining robes of his righteousness. He had paid our death by dying in our place.

That was why Jesus could accept the broken men and women of the world to his healing forgiveness. The father in his story watched for his lost son and hurried to greet him when the son came home. The son never had a chance to make the little speech he had prepared about becoming a servant in his father's house. His father's embrace swept it away in a great shout of joy.

"Son, you're home."

Now *we* can be received into God's family in just that way. But what we *cannot* do is earn our way into it. Servants earn an income, sons are welcomed home. We have to side with either the Pharisees or the cross, with earned righteousness (but it won't work for us any more than it did for the Pharisees) or free forgiveness.

Paul versus the Christian Pharisees

The battle between the religion of forgiveness and the religion of legalism carried over into the infant church. Both sides agreed that Jesus was Messiah, but the Judaizers, the Christian legalists, could not see that Jesus had abolished self-achieved righteousness. Having once been a Pharisee, Paul opposed such legalism as vehemently as Jesus had.

"You foolish Galatians! Who has bewitched you? Before your very eyes Jesus Christ was clearly portrayed as crucified. I would like to learn just one thing from you: Did you receive the Spirit by observing the law, or by believing what you heard? Are you so foolish? After beginning with the Spirit, are you now trying to attain your goal by human effort?" (Gal 3:1-3).

Legalism had not disappeared. The dragon had joined the church and was now trying to persuade everyone that Jesus had really been a Pharisee. Wherever the gospel of God's forgiveness is preached, you will always find the dragon whispering, "Yes, but . . ." Even today.

"Very well," he says, "you became a Christian by accepting God's free forgiveness and by letting him deal with your sin problem. But now that you are a Christian, you must earn the right to stay in the family. Now you must keep the law." The Judaizers taught young Christians to sing the song of grace for initial acceptance, only to revert to rule-keeping thereafter.

Paul stepped forward to answer that God's acceptance is a principle for all of life, not an admission to a legalistic treadmill. All the passion of Jesus is echoed in Paul's language. "Watch out for those dogs, . . . those mutilators of the flesh," he warned (Phil 3:2). He was referring to the Judaizers who wanted all Christian men to be circumcised as a sign of their obedience to the law. "As for those agitators," he said, "I wish they would go the whole way and emasculate themselves!" (Gal 5:12). His language is as strong as Jesus' was toward the Pharisees!

Slaves of Legalism

Jesus and Paul share the same passionate concern for those trapped by legalism. It was bad enough that the self-righteous Pharisee deceived himself, but it was worse that he deceived others. The worst thing about legalism is the pressure the legalist maintains on those around him. The stronger his personality, the more likely he or she is to gather a following of people enslaved to his system. The legalist looks holy, and people earnestly searching for holiness attach themselves to him.

For every legalist who is self-satisfied by his or her personal uprightness, there are a thousand sincere souls who by listening to his preaching and reading his books have become enslaved in the misery of legalism. For them there is no self-righteousness. Instead there is a haunted, desperate hunger for a peace with God that they can never find. The line which they must reach is painted high above them on the wall, and they are condemned to jump and jump and jump, always falling far below the standard, until they sink in weary exhaustion.

Legalism kills!

Alan and Jean were devoted members of a narrow, legalistic church. No matter how hard they worked in the church, they never really felt accepted. There were always more tasks, more duties. And because they desperately wanted acceptance, they performed them all. But it wasn't enough. Part of the game was to pretend to experience what they knew Christians were supposed to experience, but the game only increased their sense of failure.

Week by week they heard sermons that played on their guilt. They even took a strange pleasure in being browbeaten by a preacher, thanking him earnestly for stirring their oversensitive consciences to still deeper levels of self-condemnation. Alan was by now a full-blown perfectionist, but what he achieved was always so far short of what was expected. His internal tension was reaching desperate levels. The logic of legalism led him to the ultimate act of self-condemnation: he was found one morning hanging from the light fixture of their living room.

Legalism is a destroyer. The person hounded by this dragon binds himself to follow rules to win the acceptance of God and others. The answer to legalism is to see it as the enslavement it is, and to choose the grace of God instead.

The elder brother in Jesus' story accidentally gave away his total misunderstanding of his father when he exclaimed, "Look! All of these years I've been slaving for you and never disobeyed your orders" (Lk 15:29). Here was a son who thought of himself as a slave. How tragic!

Do you think of the responsibilities of Christian living as rules to live up to? You *must* have a quiet time of prayer and Bible study each day or God will take away his love from you? Is that how you find yourself thinking? Does fear drive you to obedience? Has your faith become a set of do's and don'ts (especially don'ts)?

If the answer is yes, then the dragon is keeping you from what God wants you to have as his child. The elder son could not enjoy the banquet, and a sure sign of legalism's hold on a person is the loss of joy. This dragon rules over a crowd of grim faces. "What has happened to all your joy?" Paul asked a church threatened by legalism (Gal 4:15).

Once in the great English industrial city of Manchester, where I was born, an old man lived in desperate poverty, his tiny home crowded in among squalid neighbors. He could be seen day after day combing the streets for bits of garbage, which he would put in an old brown bag he always carried. One day no one saw him. Two weeks went by before anyone worried enough to call the police. On breaking into his house, the police found it full of trash; there was no furniture except for an old bed, on which lay the old man's body. No one was surprised at this. The surprise came later when, as they tried to move the mattress, it split open and out poured a green cascade of money. He had been rich—

but he had chosen to live in poverty.

It's bad enough to live under petty rules and regulations, robbed of joy and living like a slave. But to do it when you belong to the family of God, with all the riches of his peace and joy as your heritage, is downright folly. "It is for freedom that Christ has set us free. Stand firm, then, and do not let yourselves be burdened again by a yoke of slavery" (Gal 5:1).

Take a moment to look at your Christian life. Take a joy test. If your faith has become a burden, generating a round of weary duties, then stop right now and pray, asking God to open your eyes to his truth. Examining your round of activities, determine which are done for love of God and which for other people. Are you bound by a web of rules about what you can drink, where you can go, what you must say? Paul writes in Galatians 4:9-10, "Now that you know God—or rather are known by God—how is it that you are turning back to those weak and miserable principles? Do you wish to be enslaved by them all over again? You are observing special days and months and seasons and years!"

A friend of mine spent some time in Britain's Royal Marines. He had been terrified by his sergeant-major who never missed a chance to bully and humiliate his men. But the day came when the men were discharged. They were no longer marines.

The sergeant-major's voice rang out once again: "You men there! Straighten up!"

Immediately the trained men jerked to rigid attention. Then they remembered! One by one they relaxed, hands slipping into pockets, feet scuffing the ground. They remembered their freedom, and acted on it. "Bye, Sarge," they called over their shoulder as they walked away.

We are free children of the King! We are not bound to human rules masquerading as divine law. "Therefore, there is now no condemnation for those who are in Christ Jesus, because through Christ Jesus the law of the Spirit of life set me free from the law of sin and death" (Rom 8:1).

The children of God are to be free, loving God with all their hearts and then doing for him the things that flow from love. As Augustine said, "Love God and do what you wish."

Obedience Rooted in Joy

As the dragon chains of legalism fall off, you will be ready for new direction in your Christian living. It will come through loving gratitude. Such a weak word for such a mighty concept!

Take the time to think about what God has done for you. Contemplate his love for you and where it took him. Remember his search for you, how he waited for your response. Remember the forgiveness you first knew from his hand. Look long and deeply at that love. Think of his care since then. Has he not been faithful as he promised?

He will be faithful in your present need as well. Ask God to fan the flame of your love into a great fire in response to his. Then, in that love, look again at your Christian responsibilities. Don't they look different? What seemed duties may look more like privileges now. Will time with him each day seem a duty any longer, or can you see it now as a love tryst? Even your toughest assignment may start to look like a family chore. "I died to the law so that I might live for God. . . . The life I live in the body, I live by faith in the Son of God, who loved me and gave himself for me" (Gal 2:19-20).

You will not be alone in seeking this new motivation. God's Holy Spirit indwells you and is there to help this very process. "For you did not receive a spirit that makes you a slave again to fear, but you received the Spirit of sonship. And by him we cry, '*Abba,* Father.' The Spirit himself testifies with our spirit that we are God's children" (Rom 8:15-16).

As you live in conscious communion with God, the Holy Spirit will speak to you of new things you can do to express your love for the Father. They will no longer be rules but rather opportunities to please him—not because you hope he will accept you, but because you want to express your thanks for the fact that you are already accepted.

The Bible calls this process "living by the Spirit." Paul says this about how it works: "So I say, live by the Spirit, and you will not gratify the desires of the sinful nature. . . . But the fruit of the Spirit is love, joy, peace, patience, kindness, goodness, faithfulness, gentleness and self-control. . . . Since we live by the Spirit, let us keep in step with the Spirit" (Gal 5:16, 22, 25).

We are simply to bear the fruit of what God is doing within us. I have never heard of an apple tree groaning with the effort to produce fruit. It just sits in the sun and the rain and expresses its right nature. There is a self-discipline in maintaining our life before the Lord. But when that's in place, our Christian life should be the sweet expression of our love for the Son. And what lovely fruit it is: love . . . joy . . . peace . . . patience . . . kindness . . . goodness . . . faithfulness . . . gentleness . . . self-control.

The Pharisee's Bible

Legalism distorts the meaning of God's Word. When other dragons of evil harass us, we can look to Scripture for understanding and help. But legalism has a way of twisting Scripture into a weapon against us. If we are really to be free from the legalistic trap, then we must learn how to use the Bible properly and be able to spot the legalistic tendency to approach the Scriptures as a source of laws.

The New Testament is the book of the New Covenant—that

is what its very name means. The New Covenant is God's new approach to people in Jesus, through the Spirit, in which he writes his laws on our hearts (Jer 31:33). Instead of facing a set of regulations, we have the Holy Spirit within us, and he produces a fresh and spontaneous obedience to God out of love. That is what Christian living is all about. Obedience is still the aim, but instead of obedience to the dead letters of a written code, we have obedience to the living voice of the Spirit. Paul puts it this way: "We have been released from the law so that we serve in the new way of the Spirit, and not in the old way of the written code" (Rom 7:6).

We still have the guidance of God's Word, but we read it now quite differently. Instead of searching for a set of rules in its pages, we try to grasp the spiritual principles on which it rests. The details of the text must never be taken in contradiction to the great foundational principles of New Testament thinking. While it sounds simple, just a matter of interpreting Scripture with Scripture, in fact it is revolutionary. Let's see how it works.

In his second letter to the Corinthian church Paul says some things that have become the legalist's delight:

Do not be yoked together with unbelievers. For what do righteousness and wickedness have in common? Or what fellowship can light have with darkness? What harmony is there between Christ and Belial? What does a believer have in common with an unbeliever? What agreement is there between the temple of God and idols? For we are the temple of the living God. As God has said: "I will live with them and walk among them, and I will be their God, and they will be my people."

"Therefore come out from them
    and be separate,
                    says the Lord." (2 Cor 6:14-17)

The legalist reads this in the light of laws given to maintain purity. Christian people, he or she says, are to avoid contact with unbelievers and to keep to themselves, mixing exclusively with other Christians. They are to be *separated*. These verses have been used to require Christians to avoid whatever activities the legalist regards as "worldly." In previous generations it was worldly to go to movies and dancing. Today it is more likely to be listening to rock music. Characteristically the legalist has produced a prohibition, a law of "don'ts."

Now let's look at the New Covenant principle. When God looked down at a world of sinful people, he did not withdraw from them but chose instead to move closer. He was born among us. He identified with us even to the point of becoming sin for our sakes (2 Cor 5:21).

This is the theme of the New Testament, the work of reconciliation that can only come through close and sacrificial contact. The legalist has tried to persuade us to act in direct opposition to the entire thrust of God's activity in the church! God sends us out to mix with the world that people might be saved. That is what *he* did, and we are to be like him. What use is a little pious huddle of saints, shrinking away from contact with the world to keep from defilement? How does that help fulfill God's commission to evangelize the world? The legalist's interpretation, which at first sounded so scriptural, does not fit with the totality of God's Word.

What *does* the passage mean then? It is an argument against our tying ourselves ("yoking") to the world and its view. It is not so much a demand for no contact as a warning against acceptance of its stance, an excessive involvement. Marriage with an unbeliever, for example, is obviously forbidden.

Does that interpretation fit with the central theme of the New Testament? Of course it does. To be absorbed by the world would be to deny that Christ has made any difference at all. And if we are not different, then what message have we to offer? Every page of the New Testament insists that Christians are to be in frontal opposition to the spirit of the world.

True Christianity is founded on God's act of grace to us in Christ. He involved himself in our sin-spoiled lives. He did not come to demand new efforts of self-improvement from us so that he could find us acceptable. He did not come to judge but to forgive and help us. He now calls us to live toward others with the same constructive, forgiving attitude.

A second area where legalism has caused great damage is over the divorce question. Listening to people's problems, I am often overwhelmed with strong emotions. Pity and sadness are common; fury certainly is not. But fury is exactly what I felt one day listening to a lady I shall call Sylvia.

Sylvia's husband was not merely a nonbeliever, he was a brute. After years of repeated beatings and severe sexual humiliation, she finally felt that for her children's sake she must seek a divorce. She confronted her husband, and he said he didn't care what she did. In leaving home, she made the first decision for herself in her married life. Sylvia's husband sank even lower after she left, getting into drug dealing and becoming openly associated with a local massage parlor.

About that time, Sylvia read a little book which said that God hates divorce (Mal 2:16) and that under all circumstances a Christian wife should therefore stay with her husband. It assured her of God's protection if she would go back to him. The booklet said that she could change her husband by accepting whatever he did to her and loving him throughout. It quoted 1 Peter 3:1-7 as its basis for such advice.

Sylvia abandoned her new life with her children, who had just begun to emerge from the fear they had lived with in their father's house. She told her husband that God wanted her to love him whatever he did and that she wanted to be obedient. He took her back—as a slave. For months she suffered sexual torture. She was tied up, raped and treated in ways too revolting to describe. She caught venereal disease from her husband, who had refused to abandon the massage parlor and the women he met there. Her children were forced to observe much of this and were beaten if they stepped out of the cowed condition to which they had reverted.

When Sylvia had related her story, she lifted her tearful face and asked me, "Why does God want me to go through all this? I only tried to do his will."

Angry as I was at the brutality of a man like Sylvia's husband, it was primarily the booklet that made me furious. It was willing to sacrifice people like Sylvia to a devouring Moloch in order to "keep the rule" legalistically.

Of course Scripture supports marriage. Of course God hates divorce. So does every sane person, including those going through it. But can you seriously imagine Jesus asking somebody to go through what Sylvia had gone through? The Jesus who treated victims of society with such tenderness personified the mercy of God. Read again of his gentleness to the woman taken in adultery in John 8:1-11. Can there be any doubt that in his desire to respect the biblical teaching on the sanctity of marriage the legalist has "neglected the more important matters of the law—justice, mercy, faithfulness"?

This is not a book on the biblical view of divorce, and I am not going to even begin to expound the full range of New Testament teaching about it. But this much I will say here— whatever conclusion we come to about divorce, it is essential to administer it in a spirit of mercy and understanding. Legalism neglects the spirit of the New Testament in favor of a new set of laws. Jesus made it clear that people matter more than regulations.

Let's *Not* Pass It On

Many of the people I have counseled over the years whose lives have been crippled by legalism were first caught by the dragon while children. It happens so easily. We may need to be particularly watchful in our childrearing if we ourselves were reared in a legalistic home.

Children have to be taught how to live. It is the work of many years. As parents we need to pass on the skills of living, but we must always remember that what makes the child eager to learn is largely his or her deep need for love. It is easy to use that urgent need for love as a basis for control. So we find ourselves withholding open affection because our children have not done what we wanted.

Our first task as parents is to provide the security in our love that is essential for their healthy growth. They need to know we are loyal to them, that we care for them even when they are disobedient. Only when this reassuring undergirding of affection is present and well understood by our children are we ready to teach them how to live.

God's abiding love, so accurately portrayed in the father of the prodigal, is the model for parental love. If we fail in this, we set our children on a long search for the secure love they failed to find in us. Accepting and affirming must come before discipline and training. In the absence of that love, our discipline and training are bound to be legalistic, with affection being doled out as a reward for good behavior. And the result is usually one of two extremes. The child may become a rebel or a conformist. Either way we have failed. Conformist children grow to be Pharisee parents, who begin the loveless cycle over again.

On the other hand, the family that is filled with warm affection, where children know their parents love them, provides a safe setting for training and discipline. A child who knows his parents' love can cope with the times that parents fail to be wise and good with their authority. In fact, a child secure in his parents' love can cope with almost anything.

Let's renew our efforts to raise a generation of secure children who know how to love and who know how to be loved. We need to encourage one another in this. The church should be filled with children who open naturally to God's love because they saw it in their parents.

Twelve Ways to Recognize Legalism

As a final safeguard against the Dragon of Legalism, we can learn to pick out its characteristics when we hear it being taught. We can prevent it catching us unaware.

Legalistic teaching is law oriented. The legalist loves to give a list of do's and don'ts, especially don'ts. These are not offered as helpful for your spiritual growth but as requirements for you to belong to the spiritual elite.

Legalistic groups exploit peer pressure. You find yourself subtly pressured to do things you have not chosen to do. You end up doing them to please others, not out of any conviction that God is calling you to do it for him.

Legalistic groups put great value on running down outsiders. One of the few pleasures left in the legalistic lifestyle is the dubious delight of feeling superior to others who are not in the group. This stance reinforces the stress on doing what they want you to do, lest you too end up on the outside. The threat of expulsion is a powerful tool.

Legalistic teaching is unbalanced. Certain parts of Scripture are used repeatedly, while other parts (which would have provided the balancing emphasis) are strangely ignored.

Legalistic groups are joyless. Nothing kills happiness like constant self-judgment or busy judgment of others. There is no healthy joy in the legalistic lifestyle. Fun is dangerous.

Legalistic teaching is self-righteous. The pride of achievement sooner or later marks every legalist.

Legalistic teaching proclaims God's mercy for conversion but denies it afterward. You received all the grace you are allowed once you become a Christian. After that nothing is forgiven, or only grudgingly.

Legalists never forget. Whatever you did in the past, don't count on it being forgotten. It has been stored away to beat you with next time you slip.

Legalists are terrified by the World. The World is a sea of contamination. Go too near it and you might get dirty. If you are going to evangelize, do it from a distance, preferably by shouting Bible texts to people who don't know you.

Legalists recognize no good outside themselves. Other churches which disagree with them are full of hypocrites or misguided people. There is no good in the world. If an unbeliever has done something which looks good, it was no doubt done from a corrupt motive.

Legalists are hard on women and children. Legalism is inherently a bullying philosophy. Women are especially targeted with the requirement to be silent and subdued.

Legalism is depressing. If week after week you come away from a church service feeling put down and overwhelmed by the task ahead, suspect legalistic thinking either in the preacher or in yourself.

These twelve signs mark the beast of legalism. If you recognize any of them in your life, you are in danger. Pick up your battle weapons and fight!

Questions for Individuals or Groups

1. Why does Jesus speak so powerfully and critically to the Pharisees (compare Mt 23)?

2. List the problems Jesus sees in the Pharisees' lifestyle.
What are the modern equivalents in a legalistic church?

3. What does acceptance of sinners really mean in the light of the father's acceptance of the prodigal (Lk 15)?

4. Have you personally ever experienced legalistic pressure to conform in a Christian setting? How did you handle it?
How could you handle it better next time?

5. How does grace for the unbeliever get transformed into legalistic thinking once the unbeliever becomes a believer?

6. How could legalism-induced guilt become a prime motivation in running a church? Describe the process.

7. How can gratitude to God have a full place in your life?

8. How can you develop discipline without getting legalistic?

9. What does it mean to live by the Spirit (Gal 5:16-25)?

10. What examples can you recall of Scripture abuse by legalists?

4
Overcoming Lust

Putting Sex in Its Place

Fort Lauderdale's beaches in spring become an irresistible magnet for thousands of college students who flock to soak up the sun and to meet each other. The beach becomes a seething mass of bronzed and burning bodies, minimally covered to produce maximum tan and admiration.

At night the beachfront changes as the student horde transforms itself for evening entertainment in the bars. What goes on in the bars, on the streets and later in the hotels leaves no doubt that the Dragon of Lust is well fed in America today.

I was there with sixty students who had given their vacations to a Fort Lauderdale evangelism project. What we saw remains etched on my mind. Masses of young people abandoned themselves for a week of drink and sex. Leering faces stared from slow-riding cars on the strip. A pair of drunken co-eds headed for a wet T-shirt contest, while a frightened girl slumped in a bar just wanted to go home.

But we need not wander so far from home to find traces of the Dragon Lust. I think of secretaries who are closer to their bosses than to their husbands, of wives who in their loneliness find themselves attracted to mailmen or meter readers or their husband's friends. I think of others too, lonely men driven by a desperate hunger for sex, slipping into a gay bar hoping no one sees them, risking family, career and health for a brief encounter with a stranger that leaves them as dissatisfied as ever. I think of fathers struggling to control an attraction for their own children. I think of outwardly controlled and respectable men addicted to frantic masturbation in secret. I think of old men creeping around apartment blocks, desperate for a glimpse through a window of a woman in her underwear. The list is endless, and every one on it is a slave of a dragon called lust.

This dragon has grown large and powerful in our society. It is worshiped, wooed and served on every hand. It maintains whole industries of vice and pornography. Its servants prey on the young through films and videos, and corrupt the middle-aged through magazines, vice and "mature" movies. Here is an enemy that gnaws viciously at the integrity of otherwise effective Christians, leaving them at last as empty shells. It destroys people, friendships, families and churches. Its poisonous effluent is hypocrisy.

Sex Is God's Idea
In our revulsion against all this ugliness, it would be easy to reject sex itself. But that would be rejecting God's good gift to us, for he made it—and he made it good! Sex was God's idea. What we need is a guide to the right attitude toward sex and an understanding of its appropriate place in life.

Sex enters the biblical story of beginnings early, for no sooner is Adam created than we hear God declaring that man on his own is not good. And so Eve is created, part of man and yet separate, similar yet different, not a competitor but a complement. The first masculine response to the female has all the excited characteristics with which men have regarded women ever since: "This is now bone of my bones and flesh of my flesh" (Gen 2:23).

The writer of Genesis goes on to add, "For this reason a man will leave his father and mother and be united to his wife, and they will become one flesh" (Gen 2:24).

All of us know the raw power of sex. We have felt those times when sexual attraction becomes nearly overwhelming. We are all aware that if we are to avoid being utterly dominated, we have to surround it with protective barriers. Civilization has wisely built careful warning systems that enable us to control it. We are like people tiptoeing carefully around a sleeping tiger, aware that if it awakens, the fabric of our conventions may well be ripped away. Therein lies its disturbing beauty.

Some societies have reacted to this powerful beauty with great fear. Banished from contact with polite society, the tiger is placed firmly behind bars. Modern Western society, on the other hand, has persuaded itself that the tiger is merely a pussycat, and it has set the tiger free. Our society has been mauled in consequence. Tigers, after all, are dangerous.

The question we must ask of sex is, "How can we experience its beauty to the full without being destroyed by it?" We can begin to answer this question by observing sex as God created it, for in its nature lie some clues that show us how it can be experienced in full without danger or damage.

First, *sex is linked to self-giving.* True and satisfying sex relations only come when lovers seek not their own satisfaction but their partner's fulfillment. The selfish ways of sex are ultimately unsatisfying, providing only a temporary release and quick excitement. Soon the excitement fades and the jaded palate demands other partners and more extreme sexual acts, ultimately leading to a taste for perversion.

Correspondingly, true sex always feels like self-giving. Many women have sensed the giving nature of sex strongly. Although men are more easily deceived in this area, they too know that good lovemaking comes when they are unselfish and give of themselves. The true joy of sex is the delight of self-abandonment. Sex is the act of the body which expresses the gift of a soul.

Second, and fitting as well with the original premise, *marriage is self-giving*. People who love each other find within themselves a deep desire to make commitments for the sake of the beloved. The more binding and profound the commitment, the more it suits the true lover. The beauty of the ancient wedding vow moves all but the coldest heart. "I take thee, to have and to hold from this day forward, for better, for worse, for richer, for poorer, in sickness and in health, to love and to cherish till death do us part."

This is no mere piece of rhetoric. Nor is it just a legal agreement. True lovers seek to proclaim their commitment to the world; they glory it it, and they want everyone to know. The public declarations are expressions of binding, and the man who wants to bind himself is not afraid of them. He *wants* to be bound. He is giving himself in sober commitment.

Marriage is then the ultimate self-giving. It says, "I give you all I am and all I have. I will be true to you alone and forever. In good times and bad, for all my days I am yours." When we say these words, we have in fact given ourselves, as the law recognizes.

Now we can see why sex and marriage are bound together. Sex *says*, "I give myself to you," while marriage *does* the giving. Sex is like a parable that explains marriage. Marriage is the true self-giving. Within it sex expresses that commitment a couple have publicly made in their vows to each other. Outside of marriage sex is simply a lie. It says, "I give myself to you," but denies the reality, for you are not married until you're married. Up to that moment you can still walk away. Up to that moment there is still a reservation, a part of yourself not yet given. Otherwise you would be married, and you are not.

Inside marriage, the tiger of sex is freed in all its splendor. Here, where it is at home, its power is unleashed. Sex is most free and natural within the bonds of an indissoluble commitment. Love expressed so beautifully, so powerfully, so unselfishly, grows. And the relationship deepens. The Bible itself revels in this sweet glory of married love, and sex is part of its earthy song: "Rejoice in the wife of your youth. A loving doe, a graceful deer—may her breasts satisfy you always, may you ever be captivated by her love" (Prov 5:18-19).

Sex before Marriage

When I interview couples who come for premarital counseling, I always ask them, "How are you coping with sexual temptation?" It is not easy to ask, of course, but years of counseling have confirmed that it is absolutely necessary. All too often the couple hang their heads and share a story of struggle and defeat. But the question opens the door to possible growth in their relationship, for once the issue is faced there is hope. My aim is to be able to smile at them both as they ascend the steps toward me on their wedding day and to see them smile back, knowing their smile means "We won, we made it!"

To reach that goal I ask from them both a commitment to Christian marriage and to purity as a preparation for it. Once the commitment is made, I try to help them by making them accountable, so that my painful question is repeated each time we meet. Being accountable to a friend who wants the best for your marriage can be a helpful check when the heavy breathing starts.

For couples living together, it is hard to imagine putting a halt to sexual patterns so established. It feels so strange, even like a denial of their love for each other, to separate for the months before the wedding. But in spite of the difficulties, it can be done and it is worth the cost. It really works.

Couples find that the breathing space free from sex gives them the chance to explore their relationship in other ways. Those who choose to honor God in this sacrificial way never regret it and gain real benefits when they come together in marriage.

Sex is so powerful that once it starts it dominates life together, and the necessary growth in mutual understanding comes to a halt. I have learned from couples who have come with marital problems seeking help. Many of those with sexual problems in marriage are the very ones who engaged in sex before marriage. Sex before marriage (including heavy petting) produces guilt associations for sex which do not dissipate after marriage. Our bodies and minds don't work that way. So couples who before marriage couldn't keep their hands off one another often find after they are married that desire wanes and frustration sets in. By misusing the gift God gave them, through lack of patience, the blessing in the gift was lost.

Sex and the Single Person

What I have said so far presents problems for Christian singles. Up to this point I have followed the teaching of the Old Testament, which leads to the healthy view of sex which I have just described. The norm among the Jews of Jesus' time followed this pattern, with the result that all young men were expected to marry. But Jesus' own life offers an alternative option. Jesus contradicts nothing that I have said so far, but he does add to it. Marriage is still to be "honored by all" (Heb 13:4), but the New Testament adds an extra perspective.

First, sex belongs to this life, Jesus said, and it is irrelevant to heaven where "people will neither marry nor be given in marriage" (Mt 22:30). Since the Christian is living here as a stranger and a pilgrim in preparation for eternity, sex has a temporary significance. It is not wrong or evil, as some early Christians suggested. It is simply not of ultimate importance. Many Christians would experience deep release if they could really believe that. Our value is not grounded in our sex life. We can be complete people without it. Jesus was single and satisfied—and that settles the matter.

Second, singleness is a practical calling. Jesus said specifically that some people "have renounced marriage because of the kingdom of heaven" (Mt 19:12). Paul, the veteran missionary, knew that in times of crisis there is tremendous need for singles dedicated to the work of the kingdom who are not tied down. (Read 1 Corinthians 7:1-9 for Paul's powerful plea.) The need for singles in missions is as great as ever today, but in fact the church needs singles everywhere. I can testify to the enormous effectiveness of my single friends when they get involved in the life of the church at every level.

But we have a problem. Churches have often raised marriage as an exclusive norm, implying that singles are peculiar or failures. Then we have those embarrassing evenings when condescending couples set out to matchmake among their "poor" single friends. Nor does the prejudice stop at private dinner parties. We constantly exclude singles from church life by our language without even knowing what we are doing. "Everybody come to the potluck. Bring the children."

Perhaps the ultimate injustice is to exclude singles from leadership roles on the basis of scriptural teaching meant to apply only to married men. (See Titus 1:6, for example.) The absurdity is that the apostle Paul, and even Jesus himself, would then fail to qualify for church leadership. Singles need the church's acceptance. They are on the forefront of the battle on sex, a major arena today for Satan's power. Let's make the church a place where singles are understood and honored, supported and encouraged.

Sex in a Sick Society

Car ads have displayed scantily dressed females opening car doors for as long as I can remember. Television, of course, does its best to exploit our sexual nature to promote frantic consumerism. People locked in the closed circles of Hollywood and Burbank naturally assume that all the world shares their sleazy lifestyle, and so they saturate the airwaves with sexuality. It has been rather effective. An old limerick comes to mind:

There was a young lady from Niger
Who rode, with a smile, on a tiger.
They came back from the ride
With the lady inside
And the smile on the face of the tiger.

We have loosed the tiger, and he is hunting his prey among us. The security of the family has been ripped apart as parents seek sexual thrills with others. The devastating impact of the resulting divorces on our children is a time bomb set to explode as they reach adulthood and face relationships of their own with a hopelessly inadequate parental example.

We have loosed the tiger, and he is hunting his prey among our children. Child pornography is a multimillion-dollar industry. Our city streets are home to an army of child prostitutes of both sexes. We already see the horrors of child molestation and incest rising like a suppurating tide around us. We are a society condemned to feed on our young.

How did it all happen? It began after the postwar surge of pro-marriage, pro-babies, pro-motherhood, pro-family emotion had waned, and we had elevated our feelings to the position of ultimate control. It began to show itself first in a new emphasis on sexual gratification as the major focus of marriage. Mother not only had to drive the kids home from school in the station wagon, but she had then to leap from the car and transform herself into a sex-bunny in time for her husband's return. Slowly sexual satisfaction became the *reason for* marriage instead of its expression.

From that point on, the sex act became self-justifying. "How can it be wrong when it feels so right?" a popular song asked.

How it *feels* has become the standard for behavior. Would sex be more fun with your secretary than with your wife? Then divorce your wife, marry the secretary and regain your lost youth. Are you attracted to your own sex? Then go ahead, indulge. You only live once, and who can say it's wrong when you say it is right for you? Are you attracted to children? Why not, if it feels good? You can even say, "It's good for them!"

All that we see happening around us now is simply the outworking of the basic decision to make our feelings the ultimate judge of what we should do. The glory of American freedom has degenerated into the greedy self-indulgence of a sensual society.

Where Does It Lead?
The tiger of sex let loose outside its home in marriage rampages as the Dragon of Lust. And lust is addictive. The young man who pores over sex magazines becomes in later life the businessman soaking up pornographic movies so thoughtfully provided

by hotels everywhere. The business convention becomes for him the chance to see the real thing, and before long he is cheating on his wife with a prostitute. "Hot lust that blazes like a fire can never be quenched till life is destroyed. A man whose whole body is given to sensuality never stops till the fire consumes him" (Ecclesiasticus 23:16).

The final stages of decay in society are described in the Bible with ruthless clarity. "Because of this, God gave them over to shameful lusts. Even their women exchanged natural relations for unnatural ones. In the same way the men also abandoned natural relations with women and were inflamed with lust for one another. Men committed indecent acts with other men, and received in themselves the due penalty for their perversion" (Rom 1:26-27).

How familiar and modern it all sounds!

The physical consequences of lust-addiction are obvious in the worldwide epidemic of sexually transmitted diseases. It is becoming clear that the universe is not morally neutral but that in fact it bears in itself a moral grain. If we choose to go against the grain by a promiscuous lifestyle, we pay in consequence. There is a right way to live which we neglect at our peril.

I am not implying that God sits in heaven with a big stick to beat those who do wrong. It is much simpler than that. God's nature of goodness and righteousness is written into the fabric of the universe just because he made it. The Author's personality is written in his work. The sexually transmitted diseases—herpes, AIDS and all the rest—are the result of our wrong choices in a moral universe. Evil actions lead to evil results.

None of this dragon pampering is inevitable or irreversible. As a society we can still learn and pull back from the abyss. We dare not, however, rely on the wrong methods. Christians are turning increasingly to political action to effect moral change. By all means let us legislate to limit those who exploit and corrupt, but moral legislation on its own does not address the real problem.

Ultimately we have to change the way our society thinks. As long as there is a market for the products that feed lust, just so long will they be available, no matter what our laws may say. Without changed hearts, legislative restraint of the lust business merely drives it underground. That is not enough. We must change hearts so that the addiction itself is attacked. And the place to start is in the lives of Christian men and women.

The decisive battleground for Christians of this generation is sex. We live in a world that regards sexual purity for singles as an impossible and unnecessary ideal. Lifelong commitment in marriage is considered a quaint and beautiful idea that is no longer practical, while homosexual desire is assumed to be a lifetime condition that *must* be satisfied by sexual acts.

If our generation of Christians cannot demonstrate that God's plan for sexuality can be lived out in today's world, we have no claim to a gospel of power. We put our faith on the line as we live pure lives by God's power—whether in singleness, in marriage or, if we struggle with homosexual orientation, in a celibate lifestyle.

The score in the battle so far favors the dragon. We are not winning. For sixteen years I taught in universities. Again and again young couples came to talk with me, admitting their sexual struggle and failure to live pure lives. In speaking now at Christian colleges I face the same situations. Too often I have sat with young homosexual men who are living a promiscuous lifestyle and are being tortured with their own guilt. We have all heard of evangelical leaders whose witness has been virtually destroyed by failure in purity. The fiery Dragon of Lust is active and successful in the Christian community. The good news is that in the power of the Spirit we *can* overcome it.

Gearing Up for the Dragon Fight

Jane was known as a strong Christian girl in her church group. Yes, she did dress a bit stridently perhaps, but her testimony and knowledge of the Bible won her respect. Jane had a genuine relationship with Jesus Christ, and she had received the indwelling Spirit. However, as she confessed to me, she was being destroyed by lust. Masturbating many times a day, regularly meeting strangers for one-night stands, she was a tormented soul. In the struggle with the dragon Jane was constantly defeated.

I share her story as a reminder that there is no easy solution to the problem. Jane was a real Christian. The work of God in the soul which makes us Christian does not remove our old self. It instead provides the means to defeat the old self. The struggle for victory against lust now starts.

Jane won a decisive victory over her lust. She needed all God's delivering power but also had to put out much effort of her own to break down old habits. Sometimes people are delivered from lust by a single stroke of the Spirit's power, but not always. Do not be discouraged if your victory, like hers, comes only a small step at a time and after a struggle. Keep pressing on, for victory over lust *is* possible, and through the process you will learn much of how your Lord encourages growth in wholeness in every aspect of your life.

Step One: Face Up to the Truth

The first step in defeating lust is to drag it from the shadows, to see it for what it is and to call it by its name. As long as you make excuses for sexual lust, you will be defeated. As long as you delude yourself with rationalizing, you will continue to be enslaved.

Truth is your first weapon. Use it to destroy the excuses.

"Everybody does it," "It's normal in people my age," "I've decided it's right," I can live with it," "We love each other," "No one will ever know." These and their cousins are the lies that fatten lust. Resolutely face up to the Bible's standard. Sex is for marriage only. All other uses are wrong.

Now look at your behavior in that stark light. Check out your thought life too, for Jesus said adultery could happen in thought as well as in deed. But let me add a word of caution and clarity. It is not wrong to be tempted, but it is wrong to *yield* to temptation. As Martin Luther once said, "You can't stop the birds flying over your head, but you can stop them nesting in your hair."

Sexual temptations *will* come to mind. That we cannot help. But to seek them out, to play with them, to stimulate them—these we must not do, for they are wrong. Temptation becomes lust when we nurture it and allow it to dictate our thought life, and Jesus said clearly that such willful lusting is as wrong as adultery itself.

Step Two: Make a Decision

Having seen the behavior as wrong, *decide to stop*.

Of course, you are thinking, it isn't as simple as that. But it is! It takes only the willingness to be ruthless with yourself. One young man I knew, Mark, was addicted to pornography. He seemed to be incapable of walking past an "adult" bookstore, and he passed one every day on the way to work. When he told me how helpless he was to prevent his feet from being drawn in through the door, I asked him a simple, scientific question.

"What is the range of the force, Mark?" I was deadly serious. I know well enough the sense of helplessness before overwhelming temptation, but *it always has a range*. "If you are on the other side of the street, are you drawn in?"

"Yes."

"If you are on the next block, are you drawn in?"

"No."

There was the solution. When Mark chose to walk on that block, he was in fact making the decision to enter the bookstore. He knew he had no power to resist when he was walking past the door. It was too late to fight then. So together we developed a strategy in which he walked around the bookstore at one block distance—and it worked! If you can't defeat a temptation in some situation, back up to the point where you can.

Working with an engaged couple who are being defeated in this area, I ask them where they are when it happens. In a parked car? Then when you choose to park, you are choosing to fail. Don't think you can stop it twenty minutes later when the car windows are steamed up. You have to decide that it's not safe to park anywhere private.

If you can't be in one another's apartments without falling, you must decide never to be alone in the apartment. You can choose and win, but you have to be ready to do whatever it takes and make sacrifices. That forces you to ask yourself, "Do I *really* want the victory, enough to be inconvenienced?"

The inconvenience may be considerable. Some men I know have given up good jobs because they were required to travel to other cities, and they knew they could not cope with the temptations away from home. They chose to steer clear of the dragon-infested grounds, but it cost.

Step Three: Become Accountable

The battle with lust is rarely won alone. You need the help of Christian fellowship. Enlisting a Christian friend who understands the battle and is on your side is essential to success. Begin by sharing your struggle and defeat. The Bible calls this process confession. James 5:16 says, "Confess your sins to each other and pray for each other so that you may be healed."

Choose your friend carefully. Look for a mature person, not a new Christian, and avoid legalists who might be shocked by your honesty. Although you want someone who understands the problem, don't choose a person as defeated as you are with lust. Your prayer partner should have spiritual wisdom. A Christian counselor or pastor is often a good choice, but a faithful friend who knows Scripture and obeys it (as he or she is helped through your prayer for him!) will do well.

Such a friend will agree with you about the seriousness of lust and recognize it as sin. He or she will not play down the problem, as if it mattered little since "everybody does it." You don't need any encouragement to bend the truth you have already faced up to. What you want is accountability. Your friend will keep on praying for you and keep on asking you how you are doing in regard to this sin problem. This person will encourage you when you fail and remind you of God's always-renewed grace and forgiveness and of his continuing help in enabling you to have the victory.

You may need a lifeline. Let me explain. Suppose your problem is an addiction to pornographic movies, and you have to travel to a business convention. You know the hotel will have the movies right there in the room. Arrange ahead to call your partner each night before you sleep. That's accountability. That is a lifeline. And it has worked for people in just that situation. Of course, it will take swallowing your pride to share your vulnerability with a friend, but if you really want to beat this dragon, this is the cost.

Let me add one final word on accountability. If your problem is beyond what you and a friend can bring under control, go to a professional counselor. God uses all kinds of people and their gifts to bring about healing in our lives, and we are wise if we discern when we need greater help and go for it.

Step Four: Fill Your Mind with Good Things

It takes at least a couple of months and sometimes years for a lustful mental image to fade from the mind. That is in part why the battle against this dragon is so difficult. When you make your decision to stop, you still have months of mental images in the pipeline. Still, the sooner you cut off the supply line, the sooner it will end.

Lust flourishes in the empty mind. Paul told the Philippians to fill their minds with the good: "Whatever is true, whatever is noble, whatever is right, whatever is pure, whatever is lovely, whatever is admirable—if anything is excellent or praiseworthy—think about such things" (Phil 4:8).

Begin now to refill your memory bank with pure images and crowd out the unclean images of the past. It will take effort. You may not be able to read the books that others read or see the movies that others watch. Because a new mental image may torment you for months, be ruthless. Good books and films exist, but you have to look for them. Soaking in Christian fellowship will help immensely. Go to a Bible study. Meet weekly with your lifeline partner for prayer and Bible study. As you begin to build a healthy and full Christian life, the old images will gradually fade away.

Step Five: Learn to Run

Paul tells his young friend Timothy to run from youthful lusts: "Flee the evil desires of youth, and pursue righteousness, faith, love and peace, along with those who call on the Lord out of a pure heart" (2 Tim 2:22). It is good advice. But you have to know when to run.

Never fight the enemy on ground where you are weak if you have a choice. Beat a fast retreat instead.

A friend of mine attended a business conference in Las Vegas. When he saw the long waiting line for the restaurant one afternoon, he stepped across the way into a bar offering sandwiches. Sitting and chewing meditatively on his sandwich, he suddenly realized that a velvet curtain behind the bar was rising to reveal a line of scantily dressed women. He fled. Some sandwiches just aren't worth it.

Learn your danger line. Know when you should run, and don't hesitate when the moment is on you. The longer you wait, the harsher the burn of the dragon's breath, and the longer the images will burn in your memory.

Step Six: If You Fall

You will defeat the lust dragon if you truly want to, but along the way you may be occasionally defeated. If it happens, remember that God still loves you. He knew you would fail when he chose you, and he chose you anyway. He forgives those who repent and mean not to fall again.

So bring your failure to the cross. Remind yourself of the price he paid for what you did, and lay your shame before him. Jesus came for sinners and he loves to forgive. His blood cleanses, always. Now go and praise him for forgiveness, doing all that you can to stop temptation before it becomes lust.

But what if you are failing repeatedly? What then?

Stop and rethink what you have been doing. Have you skipped some of the steps above, thinking them not necessary or too drastic? For you they weren't! Go and find someone with whom you can be honest, someone whose companionship through trouble and before the throne of God, you can appreciate. Get the help you need.

Finally, let me say something to those who find my steps in dragon fighting too tough. You are thinking that surely God should simply remove the temptation so that you will not be moved to lust. It should be effortless, surely. Frankly, God does sometimes do this, but rarely. And for good reason. First, the temptation is our good sex drive getting hooked into something wrong, whether the wrong person or the wrong timing or the wrong way. But the drive itself is good, God created it, and God is not going to remove his good gift so that we won't sin. Sex is God's idea. Lust is a misuse of that gift.

A second reason God seldom does the "quick rescue" is that his fundamental purpose with us is to build us up to be his holy people. He wants us to choose to love and serve him. People who have learned to trust him in the intense battles against temptation are his special treasures. Such people are humble, for they know their personal weakness. They know how to trust to God's power rather than their own, although they do not use that to escape responsibility for their doings. Their wills are being trained through battle. God never wastes our experiences (Rom 5:3-5).

Beyond these difficult acts of the human will lies the power of God. Our efforts would be worthless if he were not at work in us. "It is God who works in you to will and to act according to his good purpose" (Phil 2:13). This knowledge is our comfort, for it assures us that we will indeed have the victory through Christ Jesus (Rom 7:25). In time you *will* experience victory over the lust dragon. You will know that the mighty power of God himself was behind your willing for purity, and the dragon was defeated. There is no room for pride in this, only for joy. For you will have grown more like Jesus in the process.

"It is God's will that you should be sanctified: that you should avoid sexual immorality; that each of you should learn to control his own body in a way that is holy and honorable, not in passionate lust like the heathen, who do not know God" (1 Thess 4:3-5).

Questions for Individuals or Groups

1. Read Genesis 2:18-25. Why did God choose to create woman from man rather than making her a separate creation?

2. How does this creation relate to sex?

3. Why does Genesis 2:24 say "for this reason"?

4. Read 1 Thessalonians 4:1-8. How can Christian single people express their sexuality without falling into lust?

5. What should the church be doing to help Christian singles?

6. Which of the suggestions in the chapter did you find helpful in your own struggle?

7. How can your fellowship group be a resource to its members in this area?

8. How can a married person help their spouse to overcome lust?

9. How does guilt from premarital sex work to spoil sex after marriage?

10. How does self-control before marriage make you a better lover after marriage?

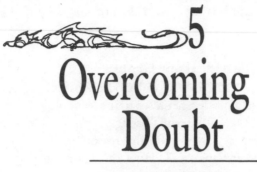

5
Overcoming Doubt

Being Confident
in a Trustworthy God

Wearing marching armor on a hot day is a decided nuisance. So it came as no surprise that the weary soldier sat down by the road and, removing his helmet, basked in the cool breeze for a few stolen moments of relief. Behind him the forest rustled with movement, and soon a sibilant voice insinuated itself into his thoughts.

"Is all this marching really necessary? Where is this elusive enemy that is so dangerous that you have to turn yourself into a walking cooking pot. Isn't it all too ridiculous? The king doesn't have to march in armor. The king doesn't march at all. Does he really know what's happening? Would he care even if he did know? Szzzzz!"

The soldier had moved quickly, and in his hand he now held the source of the voice. It was a tiny, sly, pale green dragon with a voice much more impressive that its feeble appearance. Its naked neck now hung slack, for it was dead. Doubt was its name. It has a thousand brothers—enough to plague every soldier of God and leave plenty for the company that follows behind.

But take heart, Christian. Although they are common around the entrance gate to kingdom territory, they become increasingly rare, though still dangerous, the further in you go.

The little dragon had deployed the characteristic twofold poison of doubt's attack. Personal doubt questions the King's integrity and care for his own. Intellectual doubt questions the King's information and even his existence. As Christians we must learn to fight both forms of the poison.

The Doubting Heart

Doubt has many forms. It does not strike in the mind alone. It can also bite deeply into the heart. When we lose faith in a person, it can be devastating.

I have often found in talking with people whose marriages are breaking down that the cause is loss of faith. Marsha, for example, had had an affair and was badly advised to confess all to her non-Christian husband. Until her recent adultery, their marriage had been reasonably successful. Now her guilt had brought her to her need for forgiveness, and she had come to faith in Christ. A Christian counselor had encouraged her to confess her sin to her husband, and she did. While that is sometimes good, at other times it can be disastrous; and so it proved in this case.

Marsha's husband reacted with fury, and he began an affair himself. The marriage was gone. The knowledge of her unfaithfulness had shattered his faith in her. He insisted that he could never trust her again. All her pleading that it would be different now that she was a Christian was met with stony indifference. He had simply lost faith in her.

Sometimes we lose faith in people early in life because of our parents. Take Fred, for example. He lived alone with his alcoholic mother. Fred never knew when he came home from school whether he would be met by an indulgent mother or the angry drunk who would abuse him. Nothing he could do made any difference, so he learned to withdraw. His love for his mother shriveled and died, as he became submissive but indifferent. Soon nothing touched his heart as he built up layers of protection around it.

When he got married Fred did not know how to love, because he couldn't trust any woman. His marriage was in deep trouble as his wife began to see that she had married a person with a stone heart. It took the deep ministry of the Holy Spirit over a long period of time to help him to change. It also took much determination on his part and a lot of patience from his wife. Slowly, starting with little things, Fred began to let her into his life. After a few months he broke down and poured out the story of a particular childhood incident when his mother had rejected him. For the first time Fred let her see his childhood pain. His wife listened well, and Fred realized that he *could* trust her with his inner life. From that point on progress was rapid.

For even the ordinary affairs of daily living we need human faith in one another. Without it we face, not intellectual doubt, but doubt of a personal nature. This doubt is even more damaging than intellectual doubt. It is the kind of doubt that destroys relationships. When a wife begins to doubt her husband's faithfulness, then the marriage is in danger. When we doubt God's faithfulness and cease to trust him, then our relationship with him is at hazard.

The essence of Christianity is a personal trust, not an intellectual assent. Of course, the understanding and assent are necessary. "Anyone who comes to [God] must believe that he exists" (Heb 11:6). But such mental belief is not sufficient to make me a Christian. The essential additional step is to trust this God with my life, to commit myself to obedience to his will. And that takes trust.

In the early years of this century, before people could watch television, spectacular public events were popular. A Frenchman called Blondin made a good living doing stunts as a tightrope walker. His efforts became more and more daring, and eventually before an audience of thousands he traversed a high wire over Niagara Falls. After his first crossing he coolly leaped down and declared that for his second trip he would push a wheelbarrow over the wire.

The crowd held their breath as he nonchalantly stepped out once more onto the thin wire over the plunging waters. Blondin once again made it safely across, to the enormous enthusiasm of the people. But the tension escalated still more when he announced that for his third trip he proposed to take a passenger in the wheelbarrow. The people at the front quieted down somewhat abruptly, and several melted quickly into the crowd. No one doubted that it could be done. Blondin had already wheeled the barrow across, but trusting oneself to him was another matter!

Believing in God is easy. The overwhelming majority of Americans do believe in God. But a personal commitment of my life to him is another matter entirely.

Sometimes the questions of intellectual doubt and of personal doubt come together. Thomas experienced them both. He had heard the other disciples describe their interview with the risen Christ: "Thomas, we actually saw him," they insisted.

But Thomas had trusted Jesus with his life, and his hopes had died with Jesus on the cross. He was not ready to risk disappointment a second time. "Unless I see the nail marks in his hands and put my finger where the nails were, and put my hand into his side, I will not believe it" (Jn 20:25). Now, was Thomas having intellectual doubt about the truth of the resurrection, or was he speaking as one having lost faith in Jesus personally? The answer is both. Doubts often get mixed up together just like that.

Then Jesus came. "Put your finger here; see my hands. Reach out your hand and put it into my side. Stop doubting and believe" (v. 27). Thomas looked into that familiar face and doubts fled. Plunging to his knees he said, "My Lord and my God!" That wasn't intellectual assent. It was personal surrender. And sooner or later you too need to face him. Not face an issue, but face *him*. That's what counts.

When We Are Vulnerable to Doubt

Having left England to become American citizens, my family changed its point of view on certain bits of history. The redcoats had, after all, been the "good guys," and it took some mental effort to think of them as the enemy. Our new American friends didn't always help this process. There was the sweet lady who asked one English friend, "Do the English have the Fourth of July?"

With a perfectly straight face he replied, "No madam, we go straight from the third to the fifth."

One personage of American history appears with equal frequency in textbooks of English history. His name is Benedict Arnold. It is worth remembering that Arnold was one of the best combat generals on either side in the revolutionary war, having taken a major part in capturing Ticonderoga from the British and leading the battles that preceded Burgoyne's surrender. In spite of this, Congress treated him shabbily, denying him a well-earned promotion.

Burning with resentment and inflamed with a passion for the

glamorous Peggy Shippen, Arnold became involved in graft. After all his courage and ability in the war effort, after suffering a severe wound, he had been ignored by Congress. In spite of all Washington's efforts to find him a suitable post, Arnold insisted that his commanding officer was letting him down. Hurt men are vulnerable to temptation, especially on the lips of a pretty woman. Arnold needed money, lots of it, if he wanted to move at Peggy's expensive level of society. Soon Peggy, now his wife, fanned his resentment into a bonfire of treason.

Benedict Arnold's story is an extreme case of what happens all the time. We are hurt by some real or imagined slight, and in our hurt we doubt the loyalty of those around us. The danger is that such doubt is a distorting glass through which we view all that the other person does. Take a jealous wife, for example. The more her husband tries to prove his love, the more she doubts him. If he brings her flowers, she thinks, "What has he done that he needs to bring such an expensive peace offering?" The tragedy is that once doubt penetrates our minds, it takes something very big to shake us out of our view.

Mistrusting doubt is particularly vicious with a couple who have had reason to mistrust each other in the past but who have chosen to make a new start together. For a while everything is fine. They see each other's new efforts. But time goes by and soon one of them slips a little. Immediately the other responds, "I knew it was too good to last." Rebuilding a marriage takes faith, determined faith, faith that can take a few knocks, faith that rejects the easy conclusions of doubt and keeps on trusting.

Without faith like that, a new beginning is defeated before it starts, and a couple slips back into the defensive cynicism of low expectations. If ever we are going to grow, we have to be able to survive real or imagined hurts without giving up on people.

How do we keep on trusting people when they have hurt us

and reaffirmed their trustworthiness? Maybe you have tried to forgive someone but cannot bring yourself to be vulnerable and trust that person once again. Your doubts have become a chain of negativeness which makes you always expect the worst. You believe in God, but you no longer believe in what he can do in people. Without realizing it, you have become a center for doubt in others, sapping their faith in what God can do and spreading hopelessness like a dark cloud.

Let me plead with you for a determined effort to break loose from the chains of pessimism. Be a part of the process of change in their lives by encouraging them. Refuse to give up easily, be persistent and pray for them. Have faith in people and you will be surprised how often they will live up to your high hopes. Pessimism about people is too often a self-fulfilling prophecy.

Don Quixote was mad enough to think he was a knight, and everybody laughed at his foolishness. One woman did not share in the laughter. To him she was his lady Dulcinea, to be treated with exquisite courtesy. Under his gracious treatment, she was ready to follow him to the end of the earth, and she who had been the town harlot began to behave like a lady. Don Quixote was not so mad after all.

Choose to believe in people. Try to leave a trail of encouragement behind you wherever you go. Let the space around you become a place where people behave better than anywhere else because your faith lifts them up. Naturally you'll be let down sometimes. But wouldn't you rather be an optimist who is occasionally disappointed than a pessimist who is always right?

Confronting the Dragon of Doubt

Have you ever met a cynical Christian? This person believes all the right things but never actually trusts God for his or her own life. People get like that by imagining a hurt from God. Perhaps they made a particularly important prayer request, and God did not respond as they asked. Hurt and angry, they began to doubt God personally. "I will never ask anything again. He doesn't care."

These hurt believers don't doubt God *intellectually*, but they strike back with the weapon of personal doubt. It's easy to do—and childish. Even adults can sulk when they feel hurt.

We are also vulnerable when we have neglected our relationship with God. The world's view of God is that he can be easily manipulated or bribed into doing my will by a little good behavior. As a Christian I know better, recognizing Jesus as Lord of my life, quite untouched by any petty pressures I may bring. Once I neglect my relationship with him, however, it is amazing how soon the world's view looks reasonable. Then, when I cannot bend him to my will, I sulk and declare my doubts, "just to show him."

The same shift in perspective may occur when I sin. Seeking to justify myself, I transfer the blame to God. Like the disciples in the boat, I blame it all on Jesus.

The only way to confront the whispering dragon is to face Jesus as he truly is. Fortunately, we don't have to go and find him. He is always ready to confront us.

A few days after Thomas's brave words of doubt he was facing Jesus. Thomas did not need to touch the wounds of the Master. Seeing Jesus was enough. Driven to his knees, he declared his faith: "My Lord and my God!"

In your disappointment with God are you walling yourself behind the ramparts of doubt? Then facing Jesus is the solution. Face him before you build the wall so high it becomes a prison. Take your courage in both hands and choose faith rather than doubt. Say with Job, "Though he slay me, yet will I hope in him" (Job 13:15). Come to God with all your thoughts and feelings, tell him about them, and let him take care of them all.

The letter to the Hebrews was written to Jewish Christians who were finding their faith hard going. The writer uses every argument he can to lift their eyes from their doubts to face Jesus. The author makes clear what personal doubt involves: "To their loss they are crucifying the Son of God all over again and subjecting him to public disgrace" (Heb 6:6). It is a shock treatment calculated to bring serious doubters back to reality. Do you really want to recrucify Jesus?

Let me offer one more tool to help you overcome personal doubt: *Remember your past with him.* The writer to the Hebrews calls his readers to remember their beginning faith. "Remember those earlier days after you had received the light, when you stood your ground in a great contest in the face of suffering" (Heb 10:32). Our trust in Jesus is sustained by the memories of blessings past. Recall your walk with him before you allowed doubt to spoil it. Remember your days of delight in his presence. Recall the joy of knowing peace with God and freedom from guilt. Now is God like that, or is he the gray and distant figure your doubts have made of him? *Face him and let him put it right!* The peace you once knew can be yours again.

The Proper Place for Intellectual Doubt

A key strategy of our enemy is to transform innocent creatures of our minds into nasty dragons. Doubt is one such creature. A healthy skepticism is a good and useful thing. It can be the catalyst for something rich and maturing in our lives—but not if the enemy has his way. G. K. Chesterton once noted that when men cease to believe in God, "they don't believe in nothing, they will believe anything."

As a science professor some years back, I was responsible for training bright, intelligent young people in their research for the

Ph.D. Many of them did not believe in God's existence, but they were amazingly gullible. Chesterton was right. They turned daily to the astrological column in the newspaper—and believed it! They were wide open to the latest myths of science fiction, reincarnation, psychokinesis, flying saucers, life on other planets, all without any benefit from skeptical questioning. They regularly applied careful questioning in their work, as I trained them to do, but they abandoned it in their lives.

We would see fewer human tragedies from people stepping into cults and sects, and far less exploitation of hard-earned dollars if we learned to be properly skeptical. Christians need hardheaded common sense, and insistence on reasonable proof is entirely compatible with real faith. It isn't faith that believes in fairies, it's foolishness.

The New Testament was written by men who were aware of the danger of false belief and who often confronted it. They were ready to ask for evidence and to provide guidelines for us to test the claims of others. The apostle John wrote late in his life, "Dear friends, do not believe every spirit, but test the spirits to see whether they are from God, because many false prophets have gone out into the world" (1 Jn 4:1).

Some of the tests are obvious. One girl left the Unification Church when she overheard two students at the University of Nebraska commenting on a leader of the sect as he moved along a line of his devotees. One asked the other, "Why do they worship him when he treats them like dirt?" That was all it took to open her eyes to the reality of the situation. Some beliefs are so obviously self-destructive that no more needs to be said.

Proper questioning of assertions is the beginning of finding out the truth. It is easy for us as Christians to seal ourselves off from those who differ from us and then to reassure one another that all right-thinking people think as we do. Church people do it often, carefully drawing up rules to exclude from membership all who differ with them on behavior (to dance or not to dance, to drink or not to drink), on belief (only premillennial dispensationalists welcome) and so on. Quite soon we are astonished that any Christian could ever think otherwise because all the Christians we know agree with us! We assume that our carefully controlled sample of friends is typical of the whole Christian population, which is wonderfully comforting but palpable nonsense.

Not only churches do this. The long-established bias of the media against Christianity is caused by the same problem of a self-confirming, "in" group, but in this case the view is secular liberalism. The strange world of the East Coast Establishment Intellectual is another prime example. It is time we opened our thinking to one another and made friends with people different from us. It will stretch us.

Well-functioning churches do allow a variety of secondary beliefs among their members. Of course, the members must agree on the essentials of faith and doctrine, such as on the person and work of Jesus, but they can agree to differ on nonessentials such as those mentioned earlier. Such a policy makes for a vigorous, alive church with lots of potential for arguments and therefore growth. It also demands lots of loving acceptance of people with differing views, but that is *good* for us. In fact, it begins to sound like a New Testament church! (Read Acts 15 and Romans 14 to catch the flavor of how the early church handled some differing opinions.)

The church I now serve in California has deliberately taken a policy of allowing diversity within the unity of faith. In spite of doomsayers who insisted it could not work, I am happy to report that it works very well, although it often forces us all beyond our comfort zones. We are all made to appreciate some views which we had routinely opposed. Calvinists are learning from Wesleyans, charismatics from Baptists. We are learning two things—the beauty of balance and the glory of love.

When Doubt Is Dangerous

Many Christians are untroubled by intellectual doubt and, in fact, it takes special mental effort for them to experience the healthy skepticism I have described. If you are one of these, you can be thankful that you are spared this struggle, but do not imagine you are exempt from other kinds of doubt.

For many people I have known, however, intellectual doubt is a major concern. I have known deep struggles from time to time in my own life regarding the basis of faith. This discussion of doubt is directed toward those who have wrestled for the truth and wish to slay the dragon of intellectual doubt. For the intellectual type, the great danger in our demand for reasonable evidence lies in being *unreasonably* skeptical. In fact, this very problem of when to stop asking for evidence and just to accept what is in hand has excited philosophers for the last hundred years.

At first it sounds wise to say that you will believe nothing unless it can be conclusively proven, but it is, in fact, silly. Proof cannot start until you have some sort of framework for thinking. Then proof consists in testing whether or not this new idea is consistent with what you already know. You may doubt some of the ideas you had previously accepted, but you cannot doubt them all. There is a core which you simply have to accept in order to operate. They are like the axioms in geometry.

We all believe, for example, that we are a part of a real, rational world which exists independent of us. Such a world presses itself on us the moment we are born. Of course, some philosopher could argue that it's all in our heads, a kind of giant delusion with which we deceive ourselves. We cannot *prove* that such ideas are wrong. But we choose to dismiss them as inappropriate and get on with living in the real world. So does the philosopher in practice. We are constitutionally unable to avoid accepting the reality of the world around us. We may claim that we don't, but we still continue to behave exactly like everybody else. Such claims are mere words and need not be taken seriously. Our actions reveal our opinions more truthfully than our words.

There are other things that we assume simply by being human—moral values and the freedom to respond to them, for example. We cannot help assuming that our lives, or life in general, has some sort of function or purpose. We cannot help assuming that truth is better than lies, that love is better than hate, that justice is better than oppression, that life is worthwhile. When we meet people who do not share these basic values, we regard them as sick or damaged.

Without these shared assumptions, life in general and the practice of proof in any area, scientific, religious, humanistic or artistic, is impossible. They are beyond the limits of proof. They are the framework which makes proof possible.

Now this situation is most irritating to the modern mind, which likes to have everything open to investigation, to prove or disprove, so that "mind" can reign supreme. The limits of proof limit us. It looks as if God is putting us firmly in our place, reminding us that we are creatures and not the Creator, and that there are things we cannot understand. Some questions we could not understand even if God answered them for us. Scientists have learned that some things can *never be known*. They call their rule that expresses this fact appropriately the Uncertainty Principle.

I find it rather humorous that the learned scientists, some of whom have become arrogant in their determination to reject

God, have settled on the Uncertainty Principle. It is the incongruity of our proud intellectuals meeting a brick wall in their thinking and being forced into humility. But the lesson is for all of us. Doubt has reasonable limits, and to demand proof when it is unobtainable is foolish.

The frustration of the intellectual atheist when faced with the unobtainability of proof is illustrated by Jean-Paul Sartre: "If I have excluded God, the Father, there must be somebody to invent values. If God does not exist man is forlorn for he cannot find anything to depend upon either within or without himself. I am deeply convinced that morals are both impossible and necessary." One would think that a rational response would be to abandon the denial of God's existence when it leads to such confusion.

Comparing Explanations of What Life Is

If demanding proof for everything turns out to be impossible, what do we do? The answer lies in the idea of a "world view."

While we cannot prove basic assumptions like our freedom to choose, our sense of right and wrong, or the reality of our world, we can compare explanations of how the universe came to exist and see how complete and satisfying such explanations are. We can even choose reasonably between explanations. When we find the best explanation we can, it is reasonable and logical to work with it, to accept it, until a better one comes along.

If our explanation involves the existence of God, the fact that we have accepted the explanation does not mean we have "proved" his existence. It only means that a belief in God is part of a complete and consistent explanation of life and the universe. For these explanations or world views to be effective, they need to explain why things are the way they are. The more they explain, the better they are. The more of our basic experience that a world view ignores, the more likely we shall be to reject it as unsatisfactory.

The Christian World View

The Christian explanation begins with God. Not just any God, but a personal God who has revealed himself to us. He is not an enlarged image of a human person. He is the eternal, sovereign Lord of the universe. Everything that exists, he made.

God exists on a level far beyond us and the universe he made, so that we cannot touch or see him. Nevertheless he could make us aware of him through our senses if he so chose. But there will always be more to him than we can see or touch or understand.

This God is good. Goodness is defined by what he is. Our knowledge of what is good comes from him having made us, for our consciences reflect an awareness of our Creator's nature. Because he is love, love will triumph over hate. Because he is life, life will triumph over death. So the universe is not morally neutral. Goodness, love and justice are built into it. Our natures reflect that fact.

This God has chosen to love us, and so he created us to enter into a love relationship with him. This explains why people all over the world feel a longing for him. It also explains the universal experience of the freedom to choose. God made us free so that we could love him, for only free beings can love.

A lonely man once programmed his computer to write him love letters daily. He built a voice system so that it spoke lovingly to him. But he remained lonely because manufactured, controlled love isn't love at all.

For anyone, even God, to seek love takes a willingness to risk rejection. God took that risk with all its consequences. The sad fact of history is that when we rejected him, we dragged creation down with us. That is why the world is such a strange mixture of good and evil. The evil is not God's doing. It has come from generations of humans letting loose its power as they chose evil rather than good—time after time after time. Our freedom to reject him even now is real, and the consequences are real too. We live in a spoiled world, but God continues to work patiently among us.

Because he is love and created us for himself, God speaks to us. He spoke to the patriarchs of Israel and began his great plan to win a people for himself out of lost humanity. First he worked through one nation, Israel, patiently teaching them his concern with goodness, showing them how to live. He disciplined them, trained them and prepared them for the final act of his plan.

Then at last God came himself, to take on our condition, to walk in the world we had spoiled, to confront the evil we had built up. Finally, he came to die our death, to bear the consequences of our death-choice and to win our freedom. He shattered our greatest enemy, death, and now calls all people to come to him.

That, in brief, is the Christian world view. It explains the existence of the universe, the existence of humans as free people, our awareness of right and wrong, the strange mixture of good and evil in the world, the history of Israel and the history of Christ. I know of no other world view that comprehends so much of what we know to be true in our lives so well. With a world view in place, we are ready to tackle the doubt problem.

Doubting Whether God Cares

When we doubt God's care of us, it might seem at first as if we are in the realm of personal doubt. But personal doubt usually involves intellectual doubt as well. Let's look at how this works and how we can develop an effective strategy to defeat it.

When you feel your prayer is not answered and you doubt that

God is interested in you, you need to face up to *all* that the idea involves.

If God doesn't love you, then he is simply not the all-loving God the New Testament describes. It doesn't make sense to say that he is love but he doesn't love you. So now you are facing intellectual doubt too. My advice under these circumstances may surprise you.

If you are going to doubt, doubt properly. Bring out all the implications of your doubt and face the consequences. We usually treat intellectual doubt as if it were a small, evil-smelling flower that we can plant in our mind's garden in a weak moment and allow to bloom quietly in a corner. That is not reasonable. Doubt quickly becomes a giant vine with enormous roots which, to pluck, must be pulled up roots and all. In the process you will bring your world view crashing down. For if God does not love you, then God is not love. And if God is not love, he is not good. And if God is not good, he is not God at all.

Perhaps you think he is uncaring and evil, perhaps he isn't there at all. Now you are doubting logically. Keep going. If God isn't there, how do you explain the universe with its order and beauty? How do you explain your sense of right and wrong? Without God life has no purpose, no meaning. You will have to settle for one of the confused modern world views that fail to explain any of these things. All because you decided God didn't answer your prayer!

Now you have the whole doubt before you. Now you can choose whether it is reasonable to accept it or not. Now you are doubting properly. In other words, you have to doubt the whole picture, the whole explanation of the Christian world view—or put away that doubt completely. What you cannot reasonably do is to doubt "a little" and live with it. Doubting has enormous implications. You need to know them and to count the cost before you commit yourself to doubting. And then you will not doubt.

Is this line of reasoning biblical? Yes, it is. Writing to the clever Greeks in Corinth, Paul uses exactly this technique with their doubts about resurrection.

> If there is no resurrection of the dead, then not even Christ has been raised. And if Christ has not been raised, our preaching is useless and so is your faith. More than that, we are then found to be false witnesses about God, for we have testified about God that he raised Christ from the dead. But he did not raise him if in fact the dead are not raised. For if the dead are not raised, then Christ has not been raised either. And if Christ has not been raised, your faith is futile; you are still in your sins. Then those also who have fallen asleep in Christ are lost. If only for this life we have hope in Christ, we are to be pitied more than all men. But Christ has indeed been raised from the dead. (1 Cor 15:13-20)

If you are going to doubt, doubt properly. Better still, decide that doubt does not provide a creditable alternative to the world view you already have.

Trusting When All Is Dark

Sometimes the dragon that woos us to doubt is neither intellectual nor personal in his attack. Rather, he is like a scaly dinosaur calling us into the dusty valley where his own parched bones will later be found. I have met this dragon and fought him in the valley of dryness. Some years ago I reached a point where my Christian life was utterly dry, lifeless. I was going through the motions but experiencing nothing—no peace, no joy, no assurance, no anything.

After months of this I was beginning to lose hope that it would ever end. I tried to fight the dragon intellectually, as I suggested earlier, but my doubt lay deeper. God seemed to have forgotten me. It seemed he no longer cared.

It all broke one agonizing night when I found myself confronting God with my resentment and frustration. When I had cried it all out of my system, I faced the future and made a vow. I was going to trust Jesus anyway, even if life remained a desert to the bitter end. It was then that for the first time I understood what Job meant in his despair when he cried out, "Though he slay me, yet will I trust in him." Nothing remarkable happened immediately. But gradually the barrenness faded away, and a month later the normal Christian experience was blessedly back.

Normally the Christian life does include feelings. Faith is not just being convinced of the truth of the doctrine of God. It is loving Jesus. The love is often an emotional thing, bringing conscious delight so that we sing for the sheer joy of knowing him. Sometimes it is the quiet peace of just knowing he is near. Sometimes it is a sense of awe as we pray before his throne.

But what do you do when the feelings all go? Those saints of long ago, John of the Cross and his teacher Teresa of Avila, knew the experience well and called it "the dark night of the senses." It is a time when God permits us to experience Christianity without the reward of good feelings. We moderns are a sensual people, and our feelings have become excessively important to us. The dragon knows how easily we can come to rely on them as evidence for our faith.

The Dragon of Dryness attacks us more easily if our normal style of worship is emotional, since we then experience our faith and feelings together. Sometimes we find ourselves practicing our Christianity just to enjoy the feelings themselves. It is easy to say "Jesus" over and over again, merely to work up the emotions we long for. Then we rise from "worship" feeling purged and satisfied. We may, however, without realizing it, have put our faith actually in our feelings rather than in God.

Emotion in worship is indeed desirable. Who wants a cold, emotionless adoration? The very idea is contradictory. But when our feelings become the object of our worship, we have become idolaters. And we are then most vulnerable to doubt when the feelings go.

True Christianity is not founded on feelings. Rather, feelings are the by-product of faith. When we grasp this, we can allow the dark night of the soul to be the Master's tool to purify our faith. There is no greater defeat for this dragon.

Our faith is based on the foundation of great truths. Jesus came. Jesus lived. Jesus died. Jesus rose. These are historical facts, and it is on them that our faith rests.

Let me confess that I strongly disagree with the popular chorus, "You ask me how I know he lives. He lives within my heart." It is true that through his Spirit he lives in my heart, but that is not how I know he lives.

I know he lives because "he appeared to Peter, and then to the Twelve. After that, he appeared to more than five hundred of the brothers at the same time" (1 Cor 15:5-6). The historical reality of Jesus' resurrection is proved in the same way other events are proved, by witnesses and evidence. My feelings are interesting, but they neither prove nor disprove the event. They are not reliable.

Once I accept the historical event as true and accept it in faith as applicable *to me,* then the feelings usually follow. *Feelings follow faith.* In fact, feelings work best when we forget about them altogether and simply live the life of obedience anyway. Listen to John's wise advice: "We know that we have passed from death to life, because we love our brothers. . . . Let us not love with words or tongue but with actions and in truth" (1 Jn 3:14, 18).

When we take our doubting dragons to Jesus, whether intellectual, personal or emotional, we find that the dragons too are vulnerable. But we must do our part in being honest and in being a center of trust for others. If we go on living as if God is trustworthy, we will find that he is indeed. And if we persist in trusting other people, we will enable some of them to live up to that trust.

Questions for Individuals or Groups

1. To which form of doubt are you most susceptible—doubt of the mind or doubt of the heart?

2. How have people disappointed you in the past?

How has this disappointment affected you?

3. How would you help a friend to redevelop a faith in people after he or she had learned a negative lifestyle?

4. Read 1 Corinthians 13:4-7. How are faith in people and love for people related?

5. Read John 8:1-11. Is Jesus naive in his expectations of the woman? Why or why not?

Why were the Pharisees so negative in such cases?

6. How does doubt come into your relationship with God?

7. How do you overcome it?

8. Which intellectual doubts are you most prone to?

9. How do you fight them?

10. Which books have helped you answer your doubts most effectively?

11. Read 1 John 1:1-4. Where is John's faith grounded?

Would you say his faith is opposed to knowledge—mere blind faith? Why or why not?

12. What is the evidence for your faith?

6
Overcoming Laziness

Finding Value in Discipline and Work

It was June 19, 1864, almost a year before the Civil War ended. General Grant's army had forced Lee's men to retreat toward the Confederate capital of Richmond. By this time the stand-up shooting battles were over, and the troops had learned to reduce casualties by digging in at every opportunity. The lines around Richmond were particularly well fortified at Petersburg to protect the railroad linking Richmond with the South and its crucial supplies.

In a brilliant move a group of Union soldiers who had been miners in Pennsylvania began a tunnel from their lines to a point beneath the Confederate fortifications. They carefully planted a ton of gunpowder at the end of the tunnel and retired to light the fuse.

The results were spectacular. One observer described the amazing explosion as "an enormous whirlwind." A colossal crater was created at the center of the Confederate defense system, leaving their lines completely vulnerable to any concerted Union attack.

But that was exactly what did *not* happen. No Union leader stepped in to call a charge. Instead, leaderless Union infantry milled around in the crater, sightseeing! The empty trenches were not occupied, and no attack on the reeling defenders was organized. In time Lee's invincible warriors recovered and counterattacked, pouring murderous fire into the crowd in the crater. Soon new defenses were dug, and the stalemate formed once more.

What went wrong?

General Ledlie, who had been entrusted with commanding the attack, was busy at the crucial moment opening a bottle of wine in his bombproof shelter. The slaughter of the Union soldiers in the crater had been caused by one man's laziness. His laziness was responsible too for the deaths of the thousands who died during those weary months as the war dragged on to its final end.

Laziness in the military can mean disaster, for a troop or a nation. Take Pearl Harbor, for example. On the morning of December 7, 1945, when the Zeros swooped down with death winking from their wingtips, laziness played its part in the unpreparedness of both Navy and Army units. No one was ready— in spite of intelligence alerts and even radar warnings.

Where were the army's defenses that morning? How was such a thing possible? The testimony of Charles Utterback, head foreman for the district engineers, captured the painful truth in a nutshell. "The only thing I heard that morning, sir, was 'They caught them asleep.' . . . I think I heard that comment fifty times that day."

Following the attack, the President and his staff met with key senators, and Secretary of the Navy Knox faced a furious Senator Connally. "They were supposed to be on the alert," said the senator, "and if they were on the alert. . . . I am amazed by the attack by Japan but I am still more astounded by what happened to our Navy. They were all asleep. Where were our patrols?"

Of course, we cannot blame the entire Pearl Harbor fiasco on laziness, but it was certainly one major factor. Laziness can defeat a person, a group or a whole people. He is only a sly, sneaky lizard whispering a word, "Tomorrow," in our ears, but if we listen to him, he will steal our life away. All the dreams, all the plans, all our hopes can so easily end up in dusty piles in later life, with nothing achieved but disappointment. All we have to do is sit back and laze, turn on the television and relax. We will never experience much of a spiritual struggle, for the Enemy will pass by our sleeping form with a sneer. We are no threat to him while the Dragon of Laziness holds us securely out of action. At the end we may say with Francis Thompson, "My days have crackled and gone up in smoke." The Bible addresses it as a sin. It is a dragon we must be watchful of and ready to fight.

The Sluggard

The book of Proverbs attacks sins of various sorts with the biting freshness of aphorism. Robust contempt for laziness comes through in numerous places. "You sluggard" is the not-too-endearing term it uses of the lazy.

The first problem sluggards have is that *they won't start projects*. They never get going. Maybe they have dreams, but they never do anything to get them moving toward reality. They would rather take it easy.

How long will you lie there, you sluggard?
When will you get up from your sleep?
A little sleep, a little slumber,

a little folding of the hands to rest—
and poverty will come on you like a bandit
and scarcity like an armed man. (Prov 6:9-11)
Procrastination is the child of laziness. Whenever you get a good idea, just say, "Manana, tomorrow will be soon enough," and you can be quite sure that it will not happen. We have to develop a sense of urgency about life, an awareness that its ceaseless flow passes through our open hands each day, that each moment is an opportunity to be seized. Then we can wake up and begin to make things happen.

Teddy Roosevelt, one of my favorite presidents, was so intensely energetic that he was a terror to sluggards. A British visitor once described him as "an interesting combination of St. Vitus and St. Paul." He fired brisk commands at those he wanted to see active: "Get action, do things, be sane, don't fritter your time away, create, act, be somebody."

On one occasion, after playing two sets of tennis with the French ambassador, Roosevelt suggested jogging. Following the jogging, the two worked out with a medicine ball. The President, who was not even panting, then slapped the suffering Frenchman on the back and asked heartily, "What would you like to do next?"

The ambassador was heard to reply weakly, "If it's all the same to you, Mr. President, I would like to lie down and die."

I think President Roosevelt would have liked Proverbs, if he had ever been able to sit still long enough to read it.

Take a moment to think about your life. What have you done with your good ideas, your moments of inspiration? Have they drifted by with no action? Do you need to learn a little of Teddy Roosevelt's "doctrine of the strenuous life"?

It takes a great amount of effort to overcome the distractions of our society and *do* something. Television may be our strongest temptation to be passive. We are becoming a nation of people who observe life rather than live it. We watch soap operas like addicts eager for a narcotic fix. Watching sports from our comfortable sofas, we grow fat and lazy. The amazing thing is that we know this is happening to us even as we let it happen. Edward Young said:

At 30, man suspects himself a fool;
Knows it at 40, and reforms his plan;
At 50 chides his infamous delay,
Pushes his prudent purpose to resolve;
In all the magnanimity of thought
Resolves, and re-resolves;
—and dies the same.

It is time to turn off the TV set and get going—not merely to think or to plan, but to *do* something.

The sluggard won't finish projects. Proverbs 19:24 paints a witty, scathing picture to emphasize the point. The sluggard finally starts something: he's going to eat breakfast! Watch the excitement as he raises his hand, reaches out into the bowl of fruit, buries his hand in it, then stops. His butterfly mind has moved on. There he sits, eyes glazed, hand in the fruit bowl, lost forever!

How many unfinished projects do I have around the house, things I got as far as starting but never finished? Could I be a sluggard too? Sometimes I don't finish things because I am too quick to start a new project. We need the sense of selectivity that makes us stick to a task until it is done.

One time, when Teddy Roosevelt was in the oval office discussing matters of state with a friend, his daughter Alice kept popping in and out, interrupting.

"Theodore," said his friend, "isn't there anything you can do to control Alice?"

Roosevelt replied firmly, "I can be President of the United States, or I can control Alice. I cannot possibly do both!" Those are the words of a man who knows how to focus on one thing until it's done. After we have learned to start things, we need to learn the art of finishing them. That is the harder part for most of us. Initiating projects is generally more interesting than following through on them.

The sluggard won't admit the truth about his laziness and shape up. One thing a sluggard does very well—he creates excuses for himself. "There is a lion outside!" (Prov 22:13). What a marvelous excuse! "I'd love to mend the back fence, Dear. I know it's been broken for three years. I was just about to go out and do it. Look, here are my tools! Then I saw a lion out there. Sorry, Dear. It's not my fault, you know. You wouldn't want me to get hurt, would you?"

"The way of the sluggard is blocked with thorns," says Proverbs 15:19. This translates in my modern version to "I would have loved to take the family out, Dear, but the roads were so crowded"—blocked with thorns?

It's not that the lazy feel no desire: "The sluggard craves and gets nothing" (Prov 13:4). In fact, his cravings continue because he never does anything to satisfy them: "The sluggard's craving will be the death of him, because his hands refuse to work. All day long he craves for more" (Prov 21:26).

Lazy people may be quite restless, complaining about the very things they refuse to change. Stop a moment and ask yourself what things you grumble about. How many of these irritations could you remove if you used your energy to change things rather than complain about them?

Laziness makes us powerless if we give in to it for long. Proverbs 12:24 states simply, "Laziness ends in slave labor." This was literally true under Old Testament law. A person could be sold into slavery to pay off debts. But at a deeper level it is always true. We lose our ability to control our lives if we have become passive through inactivity. Lazy people become slaves first to events and eventually to other people.

The sluggard does not contribute to other people's lives. Pity the husband or wife married to a sluggard. Marriage is a partnership, and when one partner is lazy the whole family suffers. It's hard to live in a pigsty because your partner is too lazy to share the work. Children and teen-agers who share an assigned task are only too quick to figure out who is the sluggard among them.

Laziness irritates employers and fellow employees just as much as it does living mates. Again Proverbs says it pungently: "As vinegar to the teeth and smoke to the eyes, so is a sluggard to those who send him" (Prov 10:26).

Because the lazy person does not care about other people's opinion of him, he soon becomes shameless. He doesn't care who hears him toss and turn in bed through the morning: "As a door turns on its hinges, so a sluggard turns on his bed" (Prov 26:14)

Willfully continuing in any sin seems to harden us to its ugliness unless somehow we are made to see it as others do. Why aren't sluggards repulsed by their own laziness? Why don't they change? One reason is that they are no longer seeing themselves and others correctly. They have illusions about themselves: "The sluggard is wiser in his own eyes than seven men who answer discreetly" (Prov 26:16).

A second reason, however, goes more to the heart of the problem. They don't really think much of themselves. "He who ignores discipline despises himself" (Prov 15:32). Beneath that lazy sense of superiority hides self-contempt. But even knowing that won't change anything. "I know I'm no good. Pass me another doughnut!"

Hope for the Weak-willed

If laziness is the dragon that sits on your energy and drags you under, then you need first to want to change. Proverbs holds up a mirror for you to see how you appear to others. But the reflection may depress you more than motivate you to change. What has to happen for you to really change?

This question brings us to the New Testament. Here we find a two-part answer. First, the lazy must learn zeal, and second they must discover the value of work.

Zeal, the exact opposite of laziness, is a basic part of the New Testament attitude. People with zeal *care*. Zeal puts fire in your belly. For a lazy man or woman, a dose of zeal will have the same effect as my first unknowing bite into a jalapeno chili pepper—instant action!

"Never be lacking in zeal, but keep your spiritual fervor, serving the Lord" (Rom 12:11). Christianity has about it a flavor of activism. These Christians are busy people, with lots to do. They have a sense of urgency about them. Why, it's enough to tire you out just looking at them.

I saw this energy soon after I became a Christian and began dating a Christian girl. I was lazily sitting at the bottom of the class in all those subjects at school that took any effort. In less than a year I would be taking the national matriculation examinations that English high schools require of sixteen-year-olds. I didn't care at all, but my girlfriend did. My attitude was incomprehensible to her. She started bringing the books along on our dates—and read them, right there!

A thought crossed my mind. Suppose she took the examinations and passed in every subject (as she certainly intended). Suppose I passed only one subject—or none. I was going to look foolish.

I didn't know if I could work as hard as she did (that Christian zeal!), but I started to try. And I found that her spirit was infectious. (And, no, I didn't fail the examinations.)

Where does this zeal come from? It comes from a love-commitment to Jesus Christ. That's the motivation that works. Laziness and love for Jesus are incompatible. The Bible emphasizes that when you love him you *do* things—things like keeping his commands and serving others, like bearing fruit, like preparing for his return. The ripening of Christian love always shows itself in action.

Love as I'm talking about it is not some warm gentle glow. Love is above all a commitment to action. The first step in the cure for laziness is to love in the Christian sense, and that means using the will.

If the proverbs we have looked at have come painfully close to your bones, then sit up and make some decisions. Are you a Christian? Do you love Jesus? Then let's see the fire!

Committed to God's Will

Once your will is ready for action, you need to choose obedience, for obedience gives zeal its direction. Without direction zeal degenerates to mere busyness, which can be more damaging spiritually than inactivity (see 1 Tim 5:13). It matters very much that we be zealous for good, and good is defined as God's will. Jesus said, "If you love me, you will obey what I command" (Jn 14:15).

Good! Now how do I know what he wants me to do? The Bible is *full* of instructions about how to live, and we can get busy starting to live that way. But we also need to know what special things we are to do for him. We, like Jesus, are to be about our Father's business. So what is he doing in the world? According to Jesus, the Father is a worker, and his work is with people. Ours must be too.

God is not unjust; he will not forget your work and the love you have shown him as you have helped his people and continue to help them. We want each of you to show this same diligence to the very end, in order to make your hope sure. We do not want you to become lazy, but to imitate those who through faith and patience inherit what has been promised. (Heb 6:10-12)

You show your love for him by working to help his people and doing so diligently.

Look around you at the people who are a part of your daily life. How can you become a blessing to them? How can you build them up? What can you do for them? You will find you are surrounded by work opportunities once you open your eyes and choose to become a fellow worker with God. What you will be experiencing is servanthood, and true zeal always ends up "serving the Lord."

Now that you have started, how do you keep going? You are not alone in this struggle to overcome lazy flesh. But you have a model—Jesus. His greatest title from the Old Testament was "Servant of God," and this Servant of God says to us, "Follow me."

Jesus must have walked wearily sometimes, for he kept a killing schedule. But no sick person, no brokenhearted father, no hungry soul ever found him too tired to help. Can you picture him exhausted after a fierce day serving others, now resting at last? All at once a crowd of noisy children come pushing toward him. Just what he needs, right? But the children too must be served, even though he is worn out, and Jesus chides the reluctant disciples, "Let them come."

Paul encourages the Galatian Christians, "Let us not become weary in doing good. . . . As we have opportunity, let us do good to all people" (Gal 6:9-10). Jesus says, "Follow me."

The Road to Discipline

If you are serious about following Jesus, the question of discipline comes up at once. The decision to follow him is a magnificent first step. But for the long march ahead you will need to develop new attitudes and a disciplined approach to life. Remember once again that God's Holy Spirit will be working to plant these things in your life, and the Scriptures will help you. You do not go about changing your whole life pattern alone!

Here you are lying lazily in the grass. What do you see? All around you the sod is alive with activity. See that grasshopper sawing his legs together in song? Where is that bird going with its beak full of twigs? And look down here: there's a whole line of busy workmen racing along, one behind the other, probing, pushing, intently getting on with some project. Why are they carrying those little white eggs? Where are they going?

Go to the ant, you sluggard;
consider its ways and be wise!
It has no commander,
no overseer or ruler,
Yet it stores its provisions in summer
and gathers its food at harvest. (Prov 6:6-8)

The ant has one advantage. It is made this way. It doesn't have to learn to be busy. It never had to work on its attitude. It knows no other way. But we do. For us, breaking the habits of laziness will require a new attitude of discipline. Discipline is the weapon God gives us against the dragons of both spiritual laziness and laziness in the work world. Let us turn to the first of these and expose spiritual laziness for what it is.

Spiritual Laziness

Beneath the rather innocent-appearing surface of laziness are deeper and darker strains which take us into the spiritual dimension. Spiritual laziness was known by the ugly word *sloth* in Old English. Sloth is the deep distaste for the things of God which masquerades as laziness.

Have you noticed that when you start to pray your environment becomes hostile? A fly suddenly starts buzzing and bumping against the window? Undone tasks cry out for immediate attention? And if you do manage to become aware of God's presence in spite of all this intrusion, something inside urges you to stop, as if one glimpse of God is quite enough, thank you.

All that activity is your "flesh," as the Bible calls it. It is your earthly nature. It is perfectly possible to be busy at the physical and mental levels of our lives while being profoundly lazy in the spiritual. Of course, the Enemy has tactics quite adaptable to all personality types. If your nature is less active, the Enemy may use physical laziness rather than activity to mask the spiritual sloth. The alarm goes off at six, and you turn sleepily over to silence it. Still half asleep, you now face the conflict—do you get up and read the Bible and pray, or do you nestle down in bed. Choosing laziness or, more accurately, failing to choose prayer, is sloth.

Sloth can be fought by zeal. You need to settle your priorities when you are awake enough to make a thoughtful, serious commitment. Be sensible about this. It's no good making a decision that from now on you will spend an hour a day in prayer and Bible study if you have done neither for a month. Start with ten minutes and experience some success before trying to extend it.

Discipline is the key. It is the will exerting itself to drive our lazy selves toward healthy habits. To take control of our lives we first choose what habits we want to have in place, and then choose the discipline to do them. Now if the habits become compulsive or guilt-ridden, then the discipline has become warped and unhealthy. But don't worry about that as you start out. For you right now, the discipline of a consistent time of prayer and Bible study is the right beginning.

There is no easy way to learn discipline. It is tough. You may have to be hard on yourself if sloth has been your story until now. But if you ever want to have a vital prayer life, you have to use your will and insist on beginning now. *Discipline only works in the now.*

That makes it sound as if you have to do it all yourself. Not true! The Bible insists that behind your feeble willing is the mighty will of the Father. It remains true, however, that your will does play a key role. If you are serious about loving Jesus, then you have no alternative. Regular prayer is essential. Sloth has to go.

Joy in Work

The work ethic on which so much of American prosperity is built was a gift of the Puritans. For them work was not a chore. It was an opportunity to be significant in life, to please God. It was privilege as well as duty.

When the Bible says, "All hard work brings a profit" (Prov 14:23), it refers more to personal reward than financial profit. Strangely enough, Karl Marx would agree. His admiration for the workers was one of the ethical values he picked up from his Christian environment. He was angry at the rough capitalism of Victorian England because he felt the workers were not able to keep meaning and value in their work. I speak from experience when I say that production-line work in the factory, with its mind-numbing boredom, is a great inducement to laziness.

Some work is always going to be boring. A Christian manager seeking to respect people in the workplace will do what is possible to make the job more interesting. Modern industry is working at putting value back into product creation, and this is certainly an area that Christians want to back.

But some work is still going to be boring. Marx's solutions, unfortunately, turned out to be worse than the original problem. The Christian has an alternative solution. It is not a different politico-economic system. It is a reorientation in the attitude of the worker. Christians view their jobs differently as they follow the biblical perspective on work.

First, *work is for God.* A slave in the Roman world had few rights, and in the choice of labor he had none at all. For Christians in this situation (and they were many) the apostle Paul had some startling advice: "Whatever you do, work at it with all your heart, as working for the Lord, not for men, since you know that you will receive an inheritance from the Lord as a reward. It is the Lord Christ you are serving" (Col 3:23-24).

These menial, miserable tasks, set by uncaring slave owners, were to be done thoroughly and well for a higher Master, the Lord himself.

The Lord has let you work, and how you do it matters to him. The nature of the work is secondary—Paul calls it simply "whatever you do." The attitude is everything. What a blow to our lazy excuses! Do it for Jesus—that's the attitude to work with.

Second, *work is for the family.* Most people work for their dependents. Even if you are single you are probably helping others—parents, children, friends—who depend on you. The Bible recognizes this responsibility as good, insisting that it is the norm for Christians to support their families (1 Tim 5:8).

The motivation to provide support appeals to most married men. In fact, some men who don't communicate well consider their provision for the family their principal way to express love. Unfortunately, it may not appear that way at all to the family. Many women view their husbands' work quite differently. They see it as the way men escape the home and go have their masculine fun.

Obviously, a home with these two views of work is headed for trouble. The man goes off to work full of a worthy desire to provide for his family. All through the boring day this thought keeps him going. Coming home, he expects everybody to appreciate his hard work on their behalf, but they don't. They take it for granted. (After all, his wife still thinks of his work as his fun, especially if she doesn't work herself.) As resentment builds, the motivation to work dies.

Men fail to appreciate their wives' work for similar reasons. If she works in the home, he may mentally disparage the hard and often boring work of keeping the home and rearing children. He feels that only his work is really important. Hers looks easy. (A day or two at home when the wife is away or sick is a great cure for this.) If the wife also goes out to work, many husbands fail to appreciate her contribution. She may be built up in her sense of significance and self-worth through her work, but often the husband is not impressed.

All work should be rewarded with appreciation, no matter who does it. When we cease to take one another for granted and recognize that we are all working to provide for the family, we strike a blow against laziness.

Have you sent your wife a note or gift lately to thank her for her work? When did you last let your husband know that you appreciate his labor. Are your parents supporting you at college? Have you thanked them for the work they do for you? Our attitudes about work would all improve with help like that.

Third, *giving comes from working*. Part of the sense of satisfaction that comes from even the worst job is that we can then give to help others. The early Christian church pulled into its ranks some people who had been thieves, and what Paul has to say to them is instructive for all of us. "He who has been stealing must steal no longer, but must work, doing something useful with his own hands, that he may have something to share with those in need" (Eph 4:28).

Isn't that delightful? Professional criminals usually steal because they are lazy and greedy. But these thieves have become Christians, and they have new motivation that makes them work. I can just see them coming to the meeting with their first week's wages clinking importantly in their pockets. They can hardly wait for the offering to come. Do I detect a certain swagger as the coins are flipped into the bag? It feels good to give what you have earned—that's a Christian motivation.

Fourth, *work produces community*. When we work with the same people every day, we experience a most natural and human encouragement to keep on working. We feel the wonderful sense of belonging. When offered the chance to work shorter hours, people often surprise their bosses by choosing more overtime. We see the same feelings in older workers as retirement approaches. Many dread it.

Work unites us together in the great human endeavor. We feel we are somebody as we take our place, whether by producing in the economy or in rearing children. Work gives a sense of significance and worth. Work is God's gift intended, among other things, for our satisfaction (Eccles 2:24).

Fifth, *work satisfaction comes from craftsmanship*. Joseph Conrad, who knew working people well, said, "I don't like work. No man does. But I like what's in work—the chance to find yourself. Your own reality for yourself, not others."

There is great satisfaction in making something and doing it well. What the "something" is doesn't matter. It may be a car engine, a piece of music, a lesson plan, a dinner, a sermon, a book, a computer program, a microcircuit design—the list is endless. But there is the satisfying sense of craftsmanship in them all. Craftsmanship did not disappear with the industrial revolution, nor is it disappearing in the current information revolution. It is just changing form. Craftsmanship can still be found from insurance salesmanship to shipbuilding, from child rearing to steel production. The people in each trade know it and respect it when they find it in one another. Christians above all others should be marked by craftsmanship.

The End of Apathy

We have seen why work is valuable, and now we are ready to explore motivation. _Why_ should we work? The Bible tells us that _the basic motivation for work is desire._ Let us once more listen to Proverbs. "The sluggard craves and gets nothing, but the desires of the diligent are fully satisfied" (Prov 13:4). "The lazy man does not roast his game, but the diligent man prizes his possessions" (Prov 12:27).

A major reason we want to work is to get something. Teenagers often take their first job when they realize that Dad is not going to give them a Porsche. If they want one, they will have to work for it. The genius of the capitalist society is that this is frankly recognized. The Bible too recognizes the right of possession and encourages us to satisfy such desires by working.

Recently this has come under attack among some Christian groups whose ideals lean toward community of property. Such ideals often lean toward vague yearnings of a Marxist sort.

The Bible does not promote a particular form of economics. Private property is perfectly acceptable and working for it appropriate. But generosity is vital. Sharing so that all have enough is a Christian responsibility (Acts 4:32-35; 2 Cor 8:13-14). The desire to earn is good and right, but God is concerned with what we do with what we earn. He expects us to be unselfish and generous with others and responsible to those who are dependent on us.

What then can we conclude from these verses in Proverbs? *Laziness will be overcome by increasing desire.* The lazy person's problem is that he or she doesn't desire enough. The parent who desperately wants to send his daughter to college will work hard to make it possible. The more I desire a better home for my family, the more I will work. The more deeply I feel for the needs of the poor, the harder I will work so that I can give.

The second lesson is that all my desires are to be controlled and directed by my Christian life. It is not wrong to work hard and earn money. It is wrong if my only motive is to spend it on myself in selfish pleasures.

We are to be motivated by responsibility to those who depend on us and by generosity to others. Laziness is overcome as these two motivations take hold in my life.

The final motivation for overcoming laziness is the Christian attitude toward time. From the perspective of eternal life, we have little time to live on earth. But that time is significant. Over and over again the Bible insists that we are accountable to God for every moment. I like the old King James translation of Colossians 4:5 which describes wisdom as "redeeming the time." We are called to redeem the time.

Laziness Bound

That is why laziness is a dragon. It is a sin to waste time, for time is God's precious gift to each of us. To waste time is to waste life. It is an insult to God.

Paul Yonggi-Cho (pastor of the world's largest church) was asked why the Korean church in Seoul was so effective in its growth. His answer was that Seoul was always two minutes away from destruction by the North Korean army. You use your hours well when you don't know how many of them you've got. The task facing the people of God in this sin-weary world where evil so often triumphs is overwhelmingly urgent. Each moment matters as you interact with people. There is work at hand.

I cannot put my pen down, however, without sounding a note of caution. I have met too many people for whom stressing the urgency of time is like feeding Scotch to an alcoholic. Time is short and it is valuable, but do not let it therefore become a tyrant.

Jesus had only three years for ministry, but he never hurried. Whatever time is allotted you is enough. It is enough for relationship-building and people-nurturing as well as for the work you do. When the Dragon of Laziness is conquered and bound, the victor is a free person, not one tyrannized by time or work. Time is short, but it is plentiful for what God has for you to do.

Questions for Individuals or Groups

1. In what area of life are you lazy?

2. Are laziness and activism related to personality?
How does each do damage to the Christian life?

3. What steps should each personality type take to achieve balance?
Which type are you?

4. Read Matthew 10:35-38. What is Jesus' reaction to work pressure?

5. Write down your own order of priorities.
Now take a moment to evaluate your life in practice. Are you accomplishing your priority goals? If not, why not?

6. In the light of your previous answer, rate your zeal for serving Christ.

7. What steps can you take from this chapter to change?

8. Read Galatians 6:9-10. Review your life for opportunities to do good to others. Which opportunities should you take advantage of? How will you do it?

9. How do you view your work as a Christian?
How can you apply Colossians 3:23-24 in *your* job?

7
Overcoming the Tongue

Speaking Words of Health and Praise

photograph in the New York public library shows a little man in a torn, dirty raincoat making an open-air speech. Nobody is listening. Heedless crowds move past his pointing finger, his angry voice ignored except for an occasional pitying smile.

Another picture shows the same man a few years later with a hundred thousand people hanging on his words, whipped into an emotional firestorm by his rhetoric. He speaks from a platform draped with scarlet flags bearing swastikas. His name is Adolf Hitler.

Words are powerful. Hitler's rhetoric plunged the world into war and millions died. Words can be powerful for good too. Jesus spoke quietly in Galilee, and his words have echoed for centuries. They still change lives for good.

Surely these are exceptional examples of the power of words; perhaps you are thinking that your ordinary words are not capable of either so much damage or so much healing. But perhaps they are stronger than you think.

Mary was sixteen and overweight, a tough combination to face. She handled her size by becoming the class clown. Seeking every opportunity to play the fool, she won her acceptance by her clowning. "Good old Mary," classmates would laugh. "Such a good sport, always full of jokes!" Nobody knew how desperately Mary hoped for acceptance as a real person. No one knew how often she cried into her pillow at night in aching loneliness. They only knew the class clown.

Mary fell in love one day, and the young man responded. He saw deeper into her soul than anyone ever had, and he respected what he saw. In his good favor Mary began to blossom, and bit by bit she laid aside the self-abusive behavior patterns. Soon others saw the change in her and began to treat her differently. Then one day in the milk bar she sat on a broken chair and it collapsed. The boy she loved laughed with the rest and said, "Good ol' Mary, always good for a laugh!"

That was all it took. Mary plunged back again into her old desperation.

Our words do count. *Our* words can hurt. *Our* words can damage. We can destroy lives with our tongues. Never underestimate the terrible power of the tongue, the breath of the dragon in us. "The tongue has the power of life and death, and those who love it will eat its fruit" (Prov 18:21).

The problem is that the tongue grows close to the heart, and our hearts are all too often wicked. Have you noticed that you don't need to teach children how to use hurting, ugly speech? They do it instinctively. The tongue reveals the state of the heart. That is precisely the problem.

God's Words to Us

In the Scriptures the power of the word is fully recognized. God spoke us into being, and he has spoken to us since creation in revelation, redemption and promised victory.

The Word of Creation. As we might expect in a spiritual being, God's nature is expressed through his Word. Since he is himself all goodness, his expression, his word to us, is good. This is true especially in the creation:

> In the beginning was the Word. . . . Through him all things were made; without him nothing was made that has been made. (Jn 1:1, 3)
>
> And God said, "Let there be light," and there was light. And God said, "Let there be an expanse between the waters." . . . And it was so. And God said, "Let the water under the sky be gathered to one place." . . . And it was so. And God said, "Let there be lights in the expanse of the sky." . . . And it was so. And God said, "Let the water teem with living creatures." And God said, "Let the land produce living creatures." . . . And it was so. (Gen 1:3, 6-7, 9, 14-15, 20, 24)

What a picture! Darkness, complete and ultimate. Silence, profound and deep, with God in eternal splendor. And God spoke. His word pierced the silence as light shattered the darkness.

God spoke and a billion flaming suns blazed into being. God spoke and time began. God spoke and space arched into existence.

All God's limitless power and authority lie behind his command, so that when he says "Let it be," it is so. No wonder the Bible writers stand in awe before the Word of God. His Word is power.

The Word of Revelation. The fact that our God is a speaking God emphasizes a second truth. He wants to communicate. He speaks to Adam, to Cain, to Noah, to Abraham, to Jacob, to

Moses, and to the prophets who declared, "This is what the LORD says."

The great reality is that God is out searching for men and women, speaking to them, pleading with them, commanding them, persuading them. He is the God who reveals himself in speech. That is why we have a Bible, not as a record of the opinions of men but as the Word of God.

How do you make a friend out of a stranger? You say, "Let's get together"; and then, sitting over a steaming cup of coffee, you begin to explore one another's personalities. You talk of your family and your friends, your interests, your hopes and your dreams. Gradually you paint a self-portrait in words, saying, "This is me, I want you to know me."

Our God who is seeking our friendship has done exactly this, for: "In the beginning was the Word, and the Word was with God, and the Word was God. He was with God in the beginning. . . . The Word became flesh and made his dwelling among us. We have seen his glory, the glory of the One and Only, who came from the Father" (Jn 1:1-2, 14).

God is so determined that we should know him that he painted a self-portrait in the Word. Then he clothed the Word in human flesh and put him in Mary's womb. God bared his chest and said, "Here I am, touch me and see that I'm real." And he was in Jesus, in plain view.

The Word of Redemption. Jesus spoke. Sometimes he spoke gently, as when he called the children to him. Sometimes he spoke fiercely, as when he commanded the storm to silence. Sometimes he spoke in challenge, calling for deep commitment: "Follow me." Sometimes he spoke in comfort, assuring his followers that he would always be with them. But always, when Jesus spoke, people knew that he spoke with the authority of the Father, and his words were full of grace and truth.

Jesus knew the human bondage of our alienation from God. He knew our pride and rebellion, and he knew just what to say in response. In his speaking he died, and his death spoke even more powerfully to set us free. He said, "I love you," and for his servants love sprang newly formed to life.

"This is how we know what love is: Jesus Christ laid down his life for us" (1 Jn 3:16). The cross is God's greatest speech, for in it he reveals himself as the lover of people, determined to redeem us, to heal our souls and to bring us home to live with him forever.

Has language ever framed a more glorious story? This was the news that Jesus' apostles began to spread after he had ascended. The angel told Peter on releasing him from prison, "Tell the people the full message of this new life" (Acts 5:20). The message took life and began to grow. It sprang like a joyful song from the lips of his messengers, and "the Word of God spread" (Acts 6:7).

So powerful was this word of joy that it brought new life. Peter wrote some time later, "You have been born again . . . through the living and enduring word of God" (1 Pet 1:23). The word multiplied every time it was accepted by a new person, for each new believer spoke the message afresh. Confession of the word brought redemption. " 'The word is near you; it is in your mouth and in your heart,' . . . If you confess with your mouth, 'Jesus is Lord,' and believe in your heart that God raised him from the dead, you will be saved" (Rom 10:8-9).

This Word of God has its own might and life. And our words become powerful when we speak God's Word. I have sometimes felt that preaching was really a rather silly business. Sometimes on a Sunday morning I feel "outside" myself, watching this absurd person strutting up and down a platform, pouring out words that are all too human. And I see all these hundreds of people listening solemnly and respectfully—and I wonder if the angels are laughing at the foolishness of all this human intensity.

Then I remember that God has chosen to use "the foolishness of what was preached to save those who believe" (1 Cor 1:21), and I see the weekly miracle of Christian growth as the Word is preached. What explains this extraordinary, life-changing power in preaching? Surely it does not lie in the preachers! "The word of God is living and active. Sharper than any double-edged sword, it penetrates even to dividing soul and spirit, joints and marrow; it judges the thoughts and attitudes of the heart" (Heb 4:12).

This Word is not just for preachers. It is meant to empower the speech of every believer. That is why your personal Bible study is so important, for you are developing the ability to impregnate your thinking and speaking with the fire of the Lord. The more consistently you express the thoughts and ideas of God's Word, the more frequently you will see your speech used to bring blessing to those around you. Are your words presently blessing those who hear you?

The Word of Victory. Words play a key role in the final victory of truth and righteousness. The final word in human history will not be spoken by generals or presidents; it will be spoken by Jesus. History ends when *he* declares it to be finished—and not until. *Jesus* writes "The End" on our long story of struggle and pain. The final chapter is about him.

"With justice he judges and makes war. His eyes are like blazing fire, and on his head are many crowns. . . . He is dressed in a robe dipped in blood, and his name is the Word of God" (Rev 19:11-13).

Our words will still be significant even on that great day, for "every tongue [will] confess that Jesus Christ is Lord" (Phil 2:11). Isn't that interesting? Everyone will know and speak the truth! Can you imagine how it pleases him to hear you saying it now, in a world that denies him? The words of his people are precious in his ears.

The apostle Peter sums up the purpose of our lives and tongues when he writes, "You are a chosen people, a royal priesthood, a holy nation, a people belonging to God, that you may declare the praises of him who called you out of darkness into his wonderful light" (1 Pet 2:9). Exulting in our glorious calling to be the people of God, he gives us the reason for it all—*that we may declare his praises*. That makes our tongue our glory! It will be the means by which we will fulfill our final and eternal purpose. One day all the passion of our souls' love, as we gaze on the Father of Lights, will pour forth in adoration and praise through our tongues.

The Fallen Tongue
The tragedy is that the tongue, which was made for glory and praise, is also able to destroy. James writes, "With the tongue we praise our Lord and Father, and with it we curse men, who have been made in God's likeness. Out of the same mouth come praise and cursing. My brothers, this should not be" (Jas 3:9-10). The tragedy of the tongue is nothing less than the human story of the Fall. Our words reveal the truth about us—we are fallen, and we are tragic.

This has been the pattern from the start. Newly fallen humans used their speech to organize their great endeavor. Their plan was to take God's place, which is always the aim of fallen humanity. As they worked on their huge ziggurat, or tower, they said, "Let us build ourselves a city, with a tower that reaches to the heavens, so that we may make a name for ourselves" (Gen 11:4).

God frustrated their plan by taking away their power to communicate with each other. Without a common language they could not plan, plot or work together. The Bible traces the reason for numerous languages in our world back to this point. But the tongue has continued to express evil and to do damage, of course. And we will now turn to some of the ways that the uncontrolled tongue is used by the Chief Dragon.

The Father of Lies

The most obvious sin of the tongue is truth destruction. Truth is a potent force for good. Our God is a God of truth, and his word of truth sets people free (Jn 8:32).

We live in a world dominated by lies. That is especially true in this latter part of the twentieth century when relativism has spread its cloudy web over society. Men and women no longer ask, "Is it true?" Instead they want to know, "Is it true *for me?*"

The implication is that the truth is mere opinion and that what is true for one person may be false for another. What they mean by "true" is that "it works for me." In other words, people are concerned only with the results of holding a certain opinion. Does it make me feel better? Is it more comforting? Will it win me this sale (or promotion)? Does it help me get through the day?

Much of the positive thinking which we use to motivate ourselves is based on this approach. We are asked to tell ourselves that we are the best or the most beautiful—and to believe what we are saying is true. The believing is supposed to make it come true! Much of this is merely silly. Some of it, when what we are believing has some genuine basis in truth, can be helpful. Sometimes, however, it is a retreat into a dangerous fantasy world. People persuade themselves that they are fine, generous, good Christians—without ever actually doing anything to justify the claim. The psychological trick of believing has become a substitute for effort instead of an encouragement to good works.

One example of fantasy thinking as a destructive lie is the propaganda of the gay movement. The newspaper gives the impression that the homosexual world and the heterosexual world differ only in terms of "sexual preference." It subtly suggests that the homosexual world consists of faithful couples in satisfying long-term relationships, analogous to those of happily married heterosexual couples.

The truth is starkly different. Homosexuality is overwhelmingly promiscuous. In fact, one of its basic premises is a supposed right to indulge every lustful whim. Inevitably typical homosexuals have had dozens, even hundreds, of sexual partners. This became clear recently in San Francisco when the city faced a proposal to shut down the bathhouses because of AIDS. (The bathhouses are centers for indiscriminate sexual encounters.) The spokesperson's response emphasized that this would be an attack on a fundamental of the gay lifestyle. The indulgent city authorities backed down, and the lie triumphed.

Homosexual relationships are unhappy, insecure and guilt filled, as any experienced counselor will tell you. Yet homosexuals constantly seek that one satisfying, secure relationship. It is a possibility excluded by the very sex act that is intended to seal it. Such people are trapped by the lie.

So overwhelming is the lie that they will convince themselves and those around that they are happy. Once they "come out," they have to be happy or the whole basis of their identity will come crashing down. Now they are locked into a fantasy world which makes them into two people. The outer person becomes a frenetic, brittle personality, constantly reassuring itself of its own rightness and happiness. The inner self knows the terrible truth and lives in a cell of private agony. The homosexual lie, like all lies, creates the necessity for and anguish of further lies and hypocrisy.

A second great lie in our society captures heterosexuals and homosexuals alike. It is the lie that says all our desires *must* be satisfied, and now. We saw as we dealt with the Dragon of Lust how that lie enslaves people.

Every dragon we have faced together relies on the lie and works at trapping us in a world of self-delusion. The dragons take something good, like sex, or something true, like the beauty of righteous living, and distort it through his lie into something no longer right—like lust or legalism respectively. Jesus says of the devil, "He was a murderer from the beginning, not holding to the truth, for there is no truth in him. When he lies, he speaks his native language, for he is a liar and the father of lies" (Jn 8:44).

The examples I have given only touch the edge of the possibilities of delusion. A key reason we find it so hard to escape from anger or guilt, for example, is that we cling to the lie that it is not really our fault, or that we only do it when we are forced to. We will accept any old lie to escape the responsibility for our own behavior. That is why these dragons are only defeated when we face *the truth*.

Do you know *your* lies?

Do you know the areas where *you* hide from truth because its searching light is too painful?

Lies breed lies. One who practices lies is soon able to lie with a clear and frank gaze, with conscience serene. As a teen-ager I remember achieving this level of duplicity and feeling proud of it. I did not realize how glibly lies rose to my tongue in quite unnecessary situations. After a time I scarcely knew the difference and my lies became a habit.

When I became a Christian I was brought to a sudden stop by God. He simply and humorously gave me the gift of blushing. I looked my father in the eyes honestly and lied just as I had done a thousand times before. This time, however, my cheeks blazed red and the truth was out. Only then did I realize how lying had become a way of life for me. God was showing me that he is Truth.

> No one who practices deceit
>   will dwell in my house;
> no one who speaks falsely
>   will stand in my presence. (Ps 101:7)

Children of the Lie

Hypocrisy. The Pharisees had built a whole system on one particular lie, the belief that it was humanly possible to know and to keep the perfect law of God. They dedicated their lives to sustaining the illusion that they could be completely lawful—not aware when the sins of pride and greed crept in the back door. They set out to keep the Jewish law in complete rigor, but to make success possible they began to subtly modify it: "Of course I want to look after my parents in their old age, but I made a will that all my money is dedicated to the temple. I'm sorry, but you can see that I really can't help them now" (loose version of Mark 7:11).

Again and again Jesus attacked the lie in hope of setting them free. "Woe to you Pharisees, hypocrites!" They kept the little commands, carefully taking a tenth of the herbs from their garden, wrapping it up and offering it in the temple. But they neglected the love of God and justice for the poor, said Jesus (Lk 11:42).

I find his words challenging, don't you? The poor are with us in all our great cities, and we are not doing enough to help them. Would Jesus call me a hypocrite, I wonder?

I don't want to get into an argument about the politics of how to help the poor escape the cycle of poverty. I don't know whether welfare really works, whether the states or the federal government should be responsible or what role private industry should play. What I do know is that Christian organizations have been busy doing what they could, and evangelicals have established a history of aid, through the Salvation Army, rescue missions, relief organizations and so on. Yet I wonder if we are doing enough. I wonder if I am doing enough. Financial generosity can mask an unwillingness to get personally involved. Hypocrisy is easy for all of us.

Hypocrisy is not limited to the great arenas of social injustice, to kingdoms where an Idi Amin struts in majesty before a people he has decimated. Hypocrisy can rear its dragon head on any level. We can talk as if everything is fine in our lives in public and then go to homes made miserable by our anger or our legalism or our meanness of spirit. We train our children to maintain the pretense with us and then wonder why our teenagers despise adults. As I visit Christian high schools and colleges, I am frightened at the wide extent of youthful hypocrisy. Our children can sing the hymns and speak our Christian language beautifully, but for many it is part of a game. It has no reality for them.

Where did they learn hypocrisy? Was it not in our homes, by listening to us?

Gossip. When we build the tissue of lies and develop a lifestyle of hypocrisy, we gradually come to hate and fear the truth. Then we meet people who somehow threaten the whole façade. Do they really see through it, or is it only my fear that makes me think they do?

When threatened with embarrassment we strike back, using our tongues as weapons of defense against the person that threatens us. "They are not so great themselves! Who do they think they are, anyway?"

Soon I find myself among others who feel similarly threatened, and we feel better as we confirm each other in our rectitude by tearing down the reputations of other people. There is plenty of material for gossip to work on, for we all have our failures. Gossips seize on and rejoice in the flaws and sins of others; diminishing them makes us feel taller. But what a shabby thing it is, this spreading of evil, this tearing up of decent reputations, this gossip.

LORD, who may dwell in your sanctuary?
Who may live on your holy hill?
He whose walk is blameless
    and who does what is righteous,
who speaks the truth from his heart
    and has no slander on his tongue,
who does his neighbor no wrong
    and casts no slur on his fellow man. (Ps 15:1-3)

Malice. Behind all vicious uses of the tongue lurks the glittering eye of malice. Malicious words come from hearts that hate. They belong to the kingdom of the devil. That is why we feel such an insatiable urge to pass on something we hear about another person. There is no room for malice in the kingdom of God.

Whoever slanders his neighbor in secret,
    him will I put to silence;
Whoever has haughty eyes and a proud heart,
    him will I not endure. (Ps 101:5)

Sarcasm. When I was a member of a certain youth group we began to develop a form of humor called the put-down. Winston Churchill was a past master at the put-down. Nancy Astor once said to him in irritation, "Winston, if you were my husband, I'd put poison in your coffee."

"Madam," Winston replied, "if you were my wife, I'd drink it." We laugh, and much of our humor is based on such repartee.

Our youth group lacked the wit of Churchill, but we were unwittingly hurting one another as we worked to sharpen our humor. Much of our conversation became an exchange of sarcasm. Then one day one of the quieter girls spoke out.

"If I were a non-Christian coming into this group, I would think you hated each other." For a moment we saw ourselves in this light. We looked at the truth. She was absolutely right. The whole thing had gotten out of hand and damage was being done. We began to notice that everybody laughed except the person who was slighted. And we remembered how we felt when we were the butt of the joke. Soon the exchanges stopped.

Life wasn't as funny after that—but it was healthier. Soon I found that the best laughs were those made wryly at my own expense. "A man who lacks judgment derides his neighbor, but a man of understanding holds his tongue" (Prov 11:12).

Rudeness. In northern England where I grew up, men prided themselves on bluntness. It was meant to be speaking the truth without fear or favor, but those who spoke so bluntly were often simply rude. The tongue is a hurtful weapon, and the Bible says that love is never rude. While love does indeed rejoice with the truth, it protects and is kind (1 Cor 13:4-7).

Flippancy. I once had a good friend in ministry who had a bad sense of what was fitting and a worse sense of timing. He loved to joke. No solemn moment could arise without a wisecrack. Even at a funeral he could be relied on to say the most inappropriate thing. Often flippancy arises from simply talking too much. "When words are many, sin is not absent, but he who holds his tongue is wise" (Prov 10:19). James offers this helpful advice: "Everyone should be quick to listen, slow to speak and slow to become angry" (Jas 1:19).

A bad playwright used to complain repeatedly to Oscar Wilde that he could not get his work performed. One day he asked

Wilde, "What can I do about this conspiracy of silence?"

Wilde turned to him in response: "Join it!" (which illustrates both a cruel wit and good advice in the same two words).

If words come too easily to our mouths, if we find we frequently say things that we later regret, perhaps it is time for us to join the conspiracy of silence. Let us hear James on this subject again: "If anyone considers himself religious and yet does not keep a tight rein on his tongue, he deceives himself and his religion is worthless" (Jas 1:26).

Ask yourself, "Do I use my tongue, or does my tongue use me?"

Christianity involves a major struggle with our speech habits. How are we going to get control of the tongue, so that we become the quiet, thoughtful people that James has in mind?

Taming the Tongue

We have seen the great potential for good that we humans have in word power. We have seen it modeled by God in creation and in our Lord Jesus. The contrast of the good that is possible through a godly tongue with the damage possible through hurtful words is simply a reminder of the sin nature. But the sins of the tongue can be overcome, as every dragon can be overcome, by the power of God's Spirit in our hearts. He constantly encourages us toward a holy life. Remind yourself that in his power the tongue can be controlled. It can become a vehicle for goodness and kindness.

We begin to conquer this dragon as we renew our determination to have the victory and start to change our habits. We need to pass through three stages if we want to grow in this area. We must learn to be responsible, to be responsive and to be respectful. We will look at each of these in turn.

Be Responsible. The first step for talkative people may be simply to use their tongues less. "Learn to listen," says James. First, learn to listen to yourself. Play back your conversations in your head. Ask yourself if you are talking so much that others can't get a chance to speak. Check out if you are overriding others when they want to speak because you are carried away with what you are saying. Begin to watch for cues that indicate they want to contribute to the conversation.

Second, learn to listen to others. Try to plan listening time in your conversations. Go into a conversation with a conscious desire to understand what the other person thinks. Use your speech skills to encourage them to express themselves.

If you are married, try it in your marriage. Your spouse may be astounded at the change. You are actually, seriously, listening! If you have children, try it with them. Consciously plan to ask questions to find out what they are thinking. Aim to become skilled at encouraging, patient *listening*.

I have been trying to take this advice myself. My teen-age children confronted me not long ago. Jonathan, my son who outgrew me last year, was clearly tense about something. "Dad, I need to talk to you." I was busy, but not stupid. And I guessed it was important, so I paid attention.

"Dad, you don't listen when I talk to you. It's hopeless trying to explain how I feel. You interrupt after two sentences and you think you understand, but you don't."

He was right. I know my children so well (or so I thought) that my mind leaps to what I think they are saying before they finish. Then I start reacting, arguing, disagreeing.

I looked at my daughter. She nodded, "He's right, Dad."

I looked hopefully at my wife, but she nodded silently.

What a lesson.

I had some learning to do, learning how to listen. As I began to listen, I found my children were wiser and more interesting than I thought. They had been growing into fascinating people, and I had not noticed! Since that incident I have been trying to listen carefully, and our family life has improved because of it.

Jesus said, "Therefore consider carefully how you listen" (Lk 8:18). How can we encourage ourselves to greater quietness? It helps to remember what Jesus said: "I tell you that men will have to give account on the day of judgment for every careless word they have spoken" (Mt 12:36).

That puts it in perspective, doesn't it? Are you convinced yet that your tongue needs a short leash?

We can do something else to develop responsibility in our word control. We can make a deliberate decision to honor the truth at all times.

Start with the little white lies. You don't have to say them. Find an alternative form of words. We only tell white lies out of convenience. Remind yourself that you are a child of the truth, that you are "walking in the Light," and develop a distaste for all forms of lying—even little, "innocent" lies. They are unworthy of Christ in you. When you fail, review the conversation and think what you could have said so that you are more ready next time. Confess to Jesus and let him cleanse and forgive you. Then try again.

Finally, you develop responsibility as you control what you allow yourself to hear and experience. "The discerning heart seeks knowledge, but the mouth of a fool feeds on folly" (Prov 15:14). We feed on folly when we model ourselves on foolish people. Television soap operas offer lots of opportunity for this, as do Hollywood stars in general. Who are your models? Whom do you wish you were like? Has your diet of late included much folly?

Be Responsive. After we have sincerely tried to be responsible and have experienced a few failures, we realize how difficult all this is. We see that the battle is not going to be over in a couple of rounds or a few weeks. We are tempted at this point to quit the struggle and give up on ourselves. We are discouraged when we see how deeply our wrong attitudes are embedded in our lives. Therefore remember the Source of power to change.

Our battle for control of the tongue is, after all, a part of the process "to put off your old self, which is being corrupted by its deceitful desires; to be made new in the attitude of your minds" (Eph 4:22). Paul immediately follows with this: "Put off falsehood and speak truthfully" (Eph 4:25). God is doing the changing within us, but we must consciously cooperate. He "is able to do immeasurably more than all we ask or imagine, according to his power that is at work within us" (Eph 3:20).

To control the tongue we must be responsive to the Spirit's voice within us. Listen to that voice. Is he convicting you of a hurtful conversation? Is he encouraging you to speak truthfully and lovingly? One of the things we lose as we move so noisily through our lives is our sensitivity to the Spirit's voice. Listen to him. Ask him for guidance, and expect that still small voice to whisper in your mind.

A final way to be responsive is to cultivate a praising tongue. This is our appropriate response to God's speaking. When we have listened, we naturally praise him.

Make praise your lifestyle. Fill your days with words of adoration. Thank him routinely during your day—for the food you eat, for the sun and the rain, for friends, for work. Constantly acknowledge his goodness, and his praise will be honey on your tongue. After all, that was what he made it for. "O Lord, open my lips, and my mouth will declare your praise" (Ps 51:15).

Be Respectful. The third phase of tongue control comes when I change my attitude toward people. Over and over again we need to remind ourselves that *people matter*. The only eternals in our thing-crowded lives are people. All the rest will one day burn. People go on forever.

We interact with these extraordinary beings mostly through speech. That is why it matters so much. That waitress to whom I spoke rudely today is an eternal. That junior typist in my office who was the butt of my joke (and who flushed when we all laughed) is destined for eternity. If only I could just remember to always treat people as people!

Courtesy is an old-fashioned word but a lovely one. Courteous, gracious speech is a power that often makes other people behave better. In even such small victories evil is thrust back and the Father is exalted. "A gentle answer turns away wrath" (Prov 15:1).

We grow angry when we are treated unfairly, when someone denies our worth as people. Conversely, when someone insists on treating me with respect, I calm down. I can smile again. The sun comes out.

It is time for a checkup. How is your courtesy rating? Would your friends or family rate you a courteous friend, a courteous spouse or a courteous parent? Sit back a moment and let's make some plans together. Let's devise a gentle commendation for your next interaction. That person who so unconsciously irritates you: what might you say to her tomorrow that would affirm her worth? And that one whose work usually disappoints you: how might you phrase your suggestions tomorrow so that the point is made without hurting the person? Perhaps you can think of a graceful compliment on a portion done well, a word of affirmation or thanks. Plan it now. It is rather fun, isn't it?

Perhaps the greatest compliment you can pay, one that strongly affirms the value of other people, is to give them your time by attentive listening. Yes, listening again. Listening is a major part of tongue taming, so I want to remind us all of it again.

Come, join me in the delightful business of transforming the scorch of the fiery dragonish tongue into a refreshing, soothing blessing for those around you.

Questions for Individuals or Groups

1. Read John 1:1-18. Why does John use the imagery of *word* to describe the coming of Jesus?

2. Scan your New Testament. How many different ways of speaking do you find Jesus using? What is the purpose of each?

3. Review your conversations of the last week. What was your purpose in each?

4. What was the "illusion level" in the home where you grew up? How has it influenced you?

5. How has modern society replaced truth by illusion in (a) sexual matters, (b) government, (c) personal relations and (d) church life?

6. What are the key illusions in your life?

7. How does God deal with a Christian caught in the lie?

8. Evaluate your humor style for sarcasm.

In what settings does it occur? Is it hurtful or humorous or both? Explain.

9. What advice in the chapter was most helpful to you?

8
Overcoming Pride

Nurturing a Healthy
View of Ourselves

y April 1945 the allied armies held Berlin in a ring
of steel. The might of the Third Reich was reduced to a desperate struggle in the bombed-out ruins of their once-proud capital.
At the heart of it all, deep in an underground bunker, the last
few loyalists gathered around the great leader—now reduced to
a trembling old man with the twitching glare of madness in his
eyes.

Vast armies had once roared their allegiance to him. He had
marshaled the power to challenge and defeat all of Europe, and
his warlord's shrewdness had driven his commanders to auda-
cious victory. All this had strengthened his conviction of his own
genius to the point of megalomania. He had commanded whole
armies to die for him rather than surrender, and now the cold
winds of reality had swept away his pretensions and his troops
together.

Completely possessed by the demon pride, Hitler now conceived one last display of arrogance that was, of course, impossible. In manic exaltation he issued orders as his rage turned on his own German people. "If the war is lost, the nation will also perish," he commanded. "This fate is inevitable. There is no necessity to take into consideration the basis which the people will need to continue even a primitive existence."

All industrial plants, all electrical facilities, water supplies, gas supplies, food stores, clothing stores, bridges, railroads and ships were to be blown up. Germany was to be reduced to scorched earth, the whole nation a funeral pyre to memorialize the death of Hitler's dream.

The signs of pride are not always so earthshaking, but they are always ugly. We have lifted sport heroes to near godhood, and they have drunk the nectar of adulation. A smug arrogance often dominates the professional athlete. No matter how squalid their behavior, off the field or on, thousands will still pay to watch them. We have watched tennis players of extraordinary giftedness shout obscenities at umpires, lie screaming on the court, stamp their feet and spit at reporters. Who can forget Mohammed Ali after his victory for the world championship, screaming to know who was "the greatest"? "You are. You are," newspaper reporters chanted submissively.

Pride is alive and thriving. Sports are a mirror to the national psyche. We have become addicted to swagger. We have learned to get through each day by assuring ourselves of our worth and our rights at wildly unrealistic levels. We are heading for disaster, for pride is sin. "Pride goes before destruction, a haughty spirit before a fall" (Prov 16:18).

When Pride Is Good

The carpenter smiled as he ran his hand over the smoothed and polished seat of the chair. Finished in time for her birthday, it was lovely. Every elegant line of the armchair was clean and beautiful, expressing a lifetime of craftsmanship. That night the carpenter presented his work to his bride of forty years, his face beaming with love and pride. And it was right.

For pride can be right. It is perfectly legitimate when it expresses a realistic satisfaction in a job well done—even if you did the job yourself. The apostle Paul experienced this sense of pride in his ministry. "I have great confidence in you; I take great pride in you. I am greatly encouraged; in all our troubles my joy knows no bounds" (2 Cor 7:4).

The Bible recognizes as valid the kind of pride that comes from a realistic evaluation of our own achievements. "Each one should test his own actions. Then he can take pride in himself, without comparing himself to somebody else" (Gal 6:4). The sturdy independent spirit that takes responsibility for its own life, but still knows how to be generous, is to be admired. Without such spirit our lives degenerate, and we cease to take pride in our appearance or our achievements. We simply give up.

A second example of healthy pride is the pride we feel in the accomplishments of others. Teachers are legitimately proud of their students as they see them reach new understandings and show improvement. Paul gloried in the growth he had seen in his spiritual children at Corinth by the time of his second letter. His ministry among them had founded them deeply in the Christian faith, and he was ready to boast about them to others as he appealed to them to be generous to the poor. "Show these men the proof of your love and the reason for our pride in you, so that the churches can see it" (2 Cor 8:24).

Paul is proud of the behavior of the Christians God had placed in his charge. Pride in the accomplishments of others is legitimate.

We have all experienced the good feeling of group pride when we are accepted as part of an admired company of people. We feel loyal to the group. When the group is our nation, we call it patriotism. As long as pride of country is combined with a demand that our country live up to its ideals and behave nobly, as long as patriotism is capable of loyal self-criticism, then it too is good.

But rightful pride—whether in oneself, another or "the group"—is all too easily usurped by sinful pride when we begin to be proud of the achievement merely because *I* did it or *my child* did it or *my country* did it. Then the dragon has taken over.

When Pride Is Wrong

What the Bible condemns as pride is far removed in spirit from the legitimate pride we have looked at. The pride promoted by the dragon originates, as is so often the case with sin, in untruth. It starts with a false evaluation of ourselves. Paul is again our spokesman as he writes the church in Rome: "Do not think of yourself more highly than you ought, but rather think of yourself with sober judgment, in accordance with the measure of faith God has given you" (Rom 12:3). Paul is encouraging us to overcome pride and he suggests we begin with an accurate self-evaluation.

This must be followed by a process of evaluation, aspiration, motivation and action.

In *evaluation* we determine accurately the quality of our character and our actions. *Aspiration* determines where we ought to be. *Motivation* is the drive to change from where we are to where we ought to be. In *action* we work to make this change a reality.

Motivation and action require a lot of effort, and our laziness tends to make us dislike these steps. Evaluation and aspiration, instead of being helpful and encouraging, then become irritating. After all, if I am not going to do anything, it bothers me to know that I fall short of my goals.

One bad way to avoid the frustration is to lower our goals. But that is not as easy as it sounds. When I was a science professor some years ago, I used to direct a group of students working for Ph.Ds. Most of them had dreams of one day joining the faculty themselves and of then making earth-shattering discoveries. Occasionally I had to let one of them know that he or she was failing and would not obtain the degree. It was intensely painful for such students to let go of their hopes, and yet they had to face the unfortunate reality. We face this pain whenever we have failed to evaluate correctly who (or where) we are; it hurts because lost dreams are interpreted to mean a diminished personal worth.

So we generally opt for the easier approach of self-delusion. All we have to do is exchange our accurate self-appraisal for a lie. Sometimes when I brought the bad news to my students, they would get angry, complaining of unfairness in "the system" rather than recognizing that they were not cut out for a research career. It is so much easier to reject reality. It is certainly much easier than actually trying *to be* better. We can then bask in a glow of imagined virtue without actually doing anything. This is the start of sinful pride.

Once I have welcomed this cheap illusion, the dragon leads me into a second phase of pride. Having been unwilling to let go of my dreams and having overestimated my progress toward them, the whisper in my ear now encourages me to go further. Why not upgrade my aspirations too, since I know that I am more able than others think I am? One particular research student would do this every time I challenged him with being careless in his experiments. He blandly ignored all criticism, talked even more freely of the great future ahead of him and became lazier still. Once we substitute dreams for actions, it gets easier to do it all the time.

Positive thinking now becomes highly dangerous. It really seems true that I can do anything I want to do, if only I believe in myself enough. Soon I have lost all touch with reality as I enter that golden dream world where every desire is fulfilled simply by desiring it and willing it to be so. All with effortless ease.

Now any attempt to treat us as we really are becomes an insult, and our pride must be fed by being honored by all those around us. How far we have come from the truth of sober self-estimates and the painful effort of changing ourselves for the better!

Sometimes people behave so convincingly in their overestimation of themselves that others are persuaded. Insecure people are especially open to this power of persuasion, and so the proud and the insecure tend to gravitate toward each other. A little world of illusion is created which both sides sustain to maintain their relationship. Outsiders entering this circle are a threat because they bring with them the cold draft of reality, imperiling the entire system.

Jim Jones persuaded a thousand people to accept his illusions of greatness. To sustain the community in illusion they had to retreat to the remote jungle of Guyana where reality could not reach. But no place in the world can provide an escape from truth forever; and when investigation menaced them, the entire community was persuaded that their only escape lay in suicide. The lines of bodies sprawled in the jungle clearing were a grotesque monument to the pride of Jim Jones and the sick dependence he called out in others.

The case is extreme, but it tells a universal truth about the nature of pride, the same pride that is in all of us. Its roots are lying and laziness. Proud people are touchy because they know that truth is a threat. They fight it with irritable egotism. If you won't buy into their self-illusion, you can never be their friend. The irony is that maintaining the illusion often takes more energy than the effort required to improve or change.

The Ultimate Sin

In the sweet and peaceful landscape of heaven a cancerous worm was stirring. He was a prince in glory, his rank high in the celestial counsel. But his honor and rank were insufficient for his desire. He hungered for more and soon lusted for the highest place of all.

His burning gaze swept the hosts of heaven with contempt. They were beneath his notice. But *there,* there on the throne, was the Majesty of heaven. He did not see the beauty and his heart no longer flamed with love, for corrupting pride raged like hunger within him, and he reached for the throne as if it were his by right.

Majesty could have blasted his hand and his heart, but Majesty does not work that way. Even pride and evil must bend before his will and contribute their measure of usefulness before they are granted oblivion. So the enemy was granted the role of tester, that he might prove the quality of those whom Majesty loved.

So he came to the earthly garden lusting for vengeance, with destruction in his heart and lies on his tongue. He saw the woman and slithered to her side.

"Did God really say, 'You must not eat from any tree in the garden'?"

The woman said to the serpent, "We may eat from the trees in the garden, but God did say, 'You must not eat fruit from the tree that is in the middle of the garden, and you must not touch it, or you will die.' "

"You will not surely die," the serpent said to the woman.

"For God knows that when you eat of it your eyes will be opened, and you will be like God, knowing good and evil." (Gen 3:1-5)

The Enemy went directly to Eve's aspirations and encouraged her to long for godhood. It was his own downfall, and he entrapped her in it too. Once she had lusted for that impossible dream of being like God, she viewed everything around her differently. Now she perceived God as a threat to her aspirations rather than a loving Father. Now Adam had to be persuaded to join the doomed rebellion, which went on to encompass the whole race.

We have all been born into a world in revolt against the Source of its life and hope. Our instinct is always to follow our first parents and to aspire to godhood. That is the ultimate root of all sin, and it is nothing more nor less than pride.

Sin always begins by rejecting God's clear system of right and wrong and replacing it with a system of our own creation. "Why should it be wrong to sleep together before marriage?" we ask, asserting our own views on the subject as the new standard. "Why shouldn't I choose homosexual sex? Why shouldn't I lie, cheat, steal, break my marriage vows, have an affair? Let's get rid of God's law and make up our own!" And we repeat Eve's tragic choice and reach out to take God's throne.

Pride is the raging plague in the human condition driving us along the road toward our palaces of illusion. In reality that road leads to the grave, and sooner or later we collide with Reality himself, for we are not gods but creatures.

Go into the rocks,
   hide in the ground
from dread of the LORD
   and the splendor of his majesty!

The eyes of the arrogant man will be humbled
  and the pride of men brought low;
the LORD alone will be exalted in that day. (Is 2:10-11).

The tragedy is that in attempting to live as gods we are choosing death as people. For the life of a person is maintained by God; independence is suicide. The terrible reality of our freedom means that we can, in fact, have our choice—with all its consequences. In the end we are given what we asked for: absence from God forever. Hell is the abode of those whose pride can bear no authority over them.

Religious Pride

Religious people are especially liable to pride because they are serious about trying to be good. The Pharisees, for example, were almost desperate in their determination to keep the law. The problem was that their very goodness became a platform to reach out for godhood. A Pharisee's whole aim was to be so good in God's eyes that God would be forced to grant him a place in heaven. Trying to compel God's respect is the religious form of pride.

In religious circles the perpetual temptation is to think of ourselves more highly than we ought to think. Even those who know all the doctrines of grace, who know that "salvation by works" is impossible, find that the subtle temptation of pride in their own virtues is an ever-present pressure.

Self-righteousness blooms best in churches. It's deadly blossom grows when we begin to compare ourselves with one another: is she or he more spiritual than I am? The cure for self-righteousness must be as constant as the temptation. The cure is in knowing the truth, in continuously seeing ourselves as we are (which is always a blow to pride) and seeing God in his majesty. The truth is between us and God, and there is never room for self-righteousness there.

The Faces of Pride

While it might be helpful to recognize the dragons that our Christian brothers and sisters are fighting, that is not why Scripture warns us about them. The Word of God is not a program sheet for spectators. Rather, we need to know these dragons and know how to fight them because we are their target. Our job is to beware of sin in our own lives, so that we may fight or flee from the evil that would conquer us. It is pride in ourselves that we must be alert to, not our fellow Christian's pride. So let us look at the disguises under which pride would seek to slide into our lives and penetrate their very corners.

Pride evaluates others. Pride needs to lift itself up by putting others down. We love the feeling of being superior. We love to associate with people we respect, the rich or the famous, even those we admire for the right reasons. Pride is name dropping. (You say you had lunch with Billy Graham?) Pride is impatient with "little" people who are of no use in its restless search for power.

"Do not be proud, but be willing to associate with people of low position. Do not be conceited" (Rom 12:16).

Pride is rude—except to people who are useful. By contrast, "love is patient, love is kind. It does not envy, it does not boast, it is not proud. It is not rude" (1 Cor 13:4-5). Pride is love's opposite. It would put people down, whereas love tries to help others up.

Pride is status seeking. Position in the social hierarchy is important to pride. It is careful about social distinctions of dress and behavior. It always drinks tea with pinkie outstretched or with whatever maintains the image for the chosen sphere. Pride wears only designer-labeled clothes.

The letter of James to the New Testament church is ruthless in its attack on such status seeking:

My brothers, as believers in our glorious Lord Jesus Christ, don't show favoritism. Suppose a man comes into your meeting wearing a gold ring and fine clothes, and a poor man in shabby clothes also comes in. If you show special attention to the man wearing fine clothes and say, "Here's a good seat for you," but say to the poor man, "You stand there" or "Sit on the floor by my feet," have you not discriminated among yourselves and become judges with evil thoughts?

Listen, my dear brothers: Has not God chosen those who are poor in the eyes of the world to be rich in faith and to inherit the kingdom he promised those who love him? But you have insulted the poor. (Jas 2:1-6)

Pride despises the poor. Pride does not want to be reminded of the needs of the poor. Pride wants a hard aggressive society in which it is near the top. Pride is not comfortable with obligations to help, unless it can be fulfilled publicly and without getting dirty.

Pride is racist. Racism allows pride to look down on whole races of people as inferior to itself.

Pride is boastful. It loves to make sure that all its achievements are well known. It loves prayer-and-share meetings if it can artfully include how well it has been doing in good works, prayer and Bible study. It loves to be on display.

Pride keeps track of what others owe it. Jesus said once to the host at a party, "When you give a luncheon or dinner, do not invite your friends, your brothers or relatives, or your rich neighbors; if you do, they may invite you back and so you will be repaid. But when you give a banquet, invite the poor, the crippled, the lame, the blind, and you will be blessed" (Lk 14:12-14). But pride closed its ears.

The Death of Pride

Just as pride is rooted in lies about ourselves and in false aspirations for ourselves, so humility begins with truth in these same areas.

God's goal for our lives is really quite simple. We are to be what he made us to be—loving, responsive sons and daughters of our heavenly Father. We are not to supplant him but to be his people. Our lives are to celebrate his goodness, by delighting in him, worshiping him, serving him and choosing his ways because we love him.

To live in this way means we agree to take the place he assigned us in the universe. The Bible calls such willing acceptance "submission"—the opposite of pride. In submission we renounce independence and choose consciously to depend on him. We accept his will as the very best thing.

Each of you should look not only to your own interests, but also to the interests of others.

Your attitude should be the same as that of Christ Jesus:

Who, being in very nature God,

did not consider equality with God something to be grasped,

but made himself nothing,

taking the very nature of a servant, being made in human likeness.

And being found in appearance as a man,

he humbled himself and became obedient to death—

even death on a cross! (Phil 2:4-8)

The spirit of pride revolts at such humility. Hence the struggle we experience when we bite our tongue to keep from announcing our achievements. But the Bible is insistent: "Put to death, therefore, whatever belongs to your earthly nature" (Col 3:5). "Do nothing out of selfish ambition or vain conceit, but in humility consider others better than yourselves" (Phil 2:3).

It is difficult to change our proud estimate of ourselves and our achievements. But we must if we are ever to know God and be free of pride. The truth must be allowed to do its work in us.

Lift Up Your Eyes

If you find it difficult to face the truth, try first to concentrate your vision on God. If you could really see his glory, his holiness, his majesty, his beauty, and then if you could turn your dazzled gaze back on yourself, a right evaluation of your nature would come easily. This approach helped our spiritual forefathers to assess themselves truly. Puritan Jonathan Edwards wrote, "However sensible we may be of our meanness as compared with some of our fellow creatures, we are not truly humble unless we have a sense of our own nothingness as compared with God."[1]

All our little ideas of God must be put away like childish toys. We must see him as Isaiah saw him in a temple vision. He is high and lifted up, his train fills the temple; his voice is the sound of thunder, and when he speaks the earth trembles. His holiness is pure and burning goodness, the essential inner flame of goodness such as we have never seen.

Our God is utterly sovereign. His will is the logic of the universe. It *must be* once he has spoken it. All of creation exists by his will; even evil must in the end serve his purposes. His ways are unfathomable for mere mortals, his logic far above feeble human thinking.

It is before this God we stand, exposed in our shabby selfishness, our petty meanness, our ridiculous pride. Imagine your whole life laid out before this God. Consider how you would feel if every thought, every desire, every act lay open before him. Would you not lift your eyes to him in shame and remorse? Would not your noblest acts seem small?

The Truth about Ourselves

The New Testament writers knew this God and wrote about the human condition in light of God's perfection. They knew that we are ultimately evaluated in his light. "As for you, you were dead in your transgressions and sins, in which you used to live when you followed the ways of this world and of the ruler of the kingdom of the air, the spirit who is now at work in those who are disobedient. All of us also lived among them at one time, gratifying the cravings of our sinful nature and following its desires and thoughts. Like the rest, we were by nature objects of wrath" (Eph 2:1-3).

Paul reminded his readers at Rome of the universal sinfulness of people as he quoted from the Psalms:
"There is no one righteous, not even one;
there is no one who understands, no one who seeks God.
All have turned away,
they have together become worthless;
there is no one who does good,
not even one." (Rom 3:10-12)
Paul then races on to conclude, "There is no difference, for all have sinned and fall short of the glory of God" (Rom 3:22-23).

The apostle John says it this way: "If we claim to be without sin, we deceive ourselves and the truth is not in us. . . . If we claim we have not sinned, we make him out to be a liar and his word has no place in our lives" (1 Jn 1:8, 10).

God's evaluation of human nature is the death of pride. There is no place left for it to hide. The Lord of heaven has spoken and his word is truth. We have failed as individuals and as a race. We are unrighteous. This truth ends every attempt to "be something" before God. Pious self-justification falters into silence.

Just when we bow in despair at our worthlessness, hope blazes forth. Knowing all this, seeing all our nakedness, God loves us!

Every one of the Bible passages above is followed by the same thought. As John puts it, "If we confess our sins, he is faithful and just and will forgive us our sins and purify us from all unrighteousness" (1 Jn 1:9).

Paul explains that God accepts us out of his grace, for, he says, we are "justified freely by his grace through the redemption that came by Christ Jesus" (Rom 3:24). Elsewhere he adds, "Because of his great love for us, God, who is rich in mercy, made us alive with Christ even when we were dead in transgressions" (Eph 2:4-5).

Now it is humbling enough to realize how deeply we have fallen below God's expectations for us. But it is infinitely more humbling to see that, in spite of our worst efforts, God still loves us. Here is the deathblow to pride, for we are given all the recognition and honor that pride perversely longed for but could never deserve. Why? Just because he loves us.

I wanted to be of value and found that in myself I was worthless. Then in my despair he told me I was worth more than the universe to him. So deep was his love for me that he purchased me at the price of his own blood.

Apart from him—useless and worthless.

To him—worth everything!

But he left me no room for pride. Now I experience a deep sense of worth, but only as I abandon every pretension to be anything apart from him. James 4:6 tells us that "God opposes the proud but gives grace to the humble." Who, having seen God and knowing his offer of grace, would want to hang on to the tattered rags of pride?

Beating Down a Persistent Dragon

It would be nice if, having once seen the emptiness of pride, we could relinquish it forever. Unfortunately, the Christian life is not so simple. Pride is always waiting at the door ready to make an entry.

The resolute honesty with which we assessed ourselves in the last section must become a consistent part of our lives. Our first defense against pride is to be honest enough to admit our faults and sins, and the second is to confess them as we discover them. (Sins unconfessed can recycle to feed self- justification!)

So confession must become a part of our daily prayer lives. That is why Jesus taught us to pray, "Forgive us our sins, for we also forgive everyone who sins against us" (Lk 11:4). As we confess our sins to God, we release them to his forgiving heart and they are gone. We do not beat down pride by lashing ourselves with our failures. No, we admit them, confess them and let them go. It is in the joy of forgiveness and the celebration of God's love for us that we get caught up in who he is—and forget ourselves. *That* is the true death of pride.

But it will be back the next day, and the next. And so will be the repeated experience of God's daily mercy forgiving us as we again lay the ashes of our pride at his feet. Through it all we will grow in thankfulness.

A Test for Pride

I do not want to leave the impression that we all are hopelessly trapped by the sin of pride and that we have no way of ever being free of it. Scripture teaches that we are being sanctified by the Spirit, that he is doing his work in us even now, and that we are indeed being made into the image of Christ. That is a promise of freedom from pride! But as long as we have our sin nature, which is as long as we are mortal, we need to realize our own vulnerability. Those Christians who are most alert to pride are those who least let it take hold.

Christians of the past offer us help in our war against this dragon. John Wesley's Methodists were so called because they learned his disciplined method of reviewing life at intervals to assess progress in holiness. The Puritans too took Christian growth seriously and followed a pattern of regular self-review. Jonathan Edwards, for example, compiled a list of seventy resolutions which he read once a week. And Ignatius of Loyola founded the Society of Jesus (or Jesuits) on a system of personal discipline that required self-examination also.

If these great men of faith encourage the discipline of self-review, it seems wise to listen to them. A yearly review is probably enough because it allows time for the slow process of growth. It is important to avoid unhealthy spiritual pulse-taking. Our eyes should be on Jesus most of the time, not on self.

A review should involve a prayerful assessment of our progress over the last year. It must include both positive signs of growth where they exist and signs of dragon footprints. Don't make it merely a list of failures. This should be a time of thanksgiving as well as sober thinking.

The review should lead to a set of goals for the coming year. Then pray over these goals and reduce them to a specific commitment on a practical level. For example, "to pray more" will not do. Instead we need to set reasonable but specific goals of time and frequency. It could perhaps be "to pray twenty minutes a day, five days a week." The more specific the goals, the more likely they are to be achieved. General unfocused goals only lead to general unfocused guilt, which helps nobody.

My goals should include what I intend this year in my relationships to others, my family for starters. I need to share some of my goals with them so that I become accountable. This can be a tremendous influence for good as my spouse and children see me trying to be a better person.

Once I start the process, I have a ready-made basis for next year's review. And I can follow the evaluation with the rest of the cycle—aspiration, motivation and action.

The suggested questions which I include here may help you with the review process. Don't use them as your questions. Consider them examples of the type of thing to ask yourself.

1. Am I honest, or do I consciously or unconsciously create the impression of being better than I am? Do I exaggerate?

2. Can I be trusted? Do I pass on confidences?

3. Do I handle faithfully money or things that belong to others? Am I regularly giving generously to God?

4. Am I self-pitying or self-justifying? Can I take constructive criticism, especially from family?

5. Am I getting into the Bible by daily reading? Is the Book alive to me?

6. Is my daily prayer life satisfying, joyful and rich?

7. When did I last speak to someone with the aim of winning him or her for Christ?

8. Am I disobedient to God? Am I resentful of the authorities in my life?

9. Is there anyone at whom I feel bitter or angry or resentful? If so, what am I doing about it?

10. Is my life ordered? Am I handling priorities properly?

11. Am I defeated in any part of my life by jealousy, impurity, critical spirit, irritability, anger, distrust?

Humility and Servanthood

You can recognize in any fellowship the persons who have a spirit of humility. They are the ones who take on the role of servant to others. Jesus taught his disciples and us in the upper room just what it means to love one another.

Jesus knew that the Father had put all things under his power, and that he had come from God and was returning to God;

so he got up from the meal, took off his outer clothing, and wrapped a towel around his waist. After that, he poured water into a basin and began to wash his disciples' feet, drying them with the towel that was wrapped around him. . . .

When he had finished washing their feet, he put on his clothes and returned to his place. "Do you understand what I have done for you?" he asked them. "You call me 'Teacher' and 'Lord,' and rightly so, for that is what I am. Now that I, your Lord and Teacher, have washed your feet, you also should wash one another's feet. I have set you an example that you should do as I have done for you." (Jn 13:3-5, 12-15)

Jesus knew his own power and chose to use it in service. That is humility. It is the willingness to use our authority for others by serving them and not "lording" it over them. All leadership is to be exercised in humble service. (Elders, pastors and parents, take note.) This is to be the flavor of the Christian church. Permeating every meeting should be an eager desire to be a blessing for others. In such an atmosphere pride withers and dies.

Unfortunately, in a star-struck society people are looking for heroes to lift to a pedestal, even in the church. And they often find Christian leaders who are willing to play the game. It is all too easy for an individual to gain personal power by using his or her gifts of communication and then to become puffed up with pride because of the adulation he has received. Such leaders then place themselves above the rules and make shipwreck of their souls and the souls of their immature followers.

While the problem is real, I must be quick to point out that not all gifted leaders in the church allow this to happen to them, by any means. We are wrong to assume that all people with extraordinary gifts are full of pride just because of their success. In fact, I have been deeply impressed with the humility of the few great preachers that I have met. That they have not fallen to pride, however, is a tribute to their conscientiously having fought the temptation. It is not that they never met the dragon.

Some have thought that a new church structure might eliminate the hero-worship syndrome. I have heard people express a preference for small churches with less gifted leaders as a way of avoiding the dangers of pride. As if pride were not found in small churches! But a structure cannot eliminate an attitude problem, and ten elders can behave just as proudly as one preacher. A structure could, however, deny the expression of an extraordinary gift that God has given to some individuals. It is hard to take seriously the idea that a Spurgeon should only be permitted to preach once a quarter while mediocre preachers occupy the pulpit. The church pays a heavy price for such policies, and we are all the losers.

No, let the gifts God has given be used fully to the blessing of all. But let us all help the gifted individual to behave with humility. This cannot be done by structures and rules, but through mutual love and prayer. Highly gifted people need our prayers. They also need mature followers who know how to love preachers without idolizing them. A church structure that provides accountability can be a help.

We need to remind ourselves that the gifts God gives are not marks of esteem but acts of grace. Great skill in music or preaching does not mean that the person is better than others. Remember Mozart, whose musical gifts were amazing but whose personal behavior was often bizarre. We do not help people by lionizing them. Loving them means being honest with them and by serving them with whatever gifts we have.

We need also to remind ourselves that the gifts do not in fact belong to the person. They are given to the church for the common good. Let us honor men and women who combine giftedness with humility, for they may be honored safely. Those who are close to Billy Graham and Chuck Swindoll, for example, testify to the genuineness of their humble spirits. We all can testify to their giftedness.

Unfortunately, we don't have to be highly esteemed to feel the temptation. God has given each of us in the body a gift to use for others. The temptation touches us all. So we can all draw a lesson from the discussion. Pride tempts us to treat our gifts as private property which exalt our status. This pride can and must be routed by developing a true servant's heart. Gifts then become released to minister, and no more to our credit than possessing blue eyes.

It all comes back, as it must, to love. Love is self-forgetful and ready to serve. When love flourishes, pride dies. Let me close our thoughts on pride with a word from Jonathan Edwards's book, *Charity and Its Fruits:*

Renounce all glory except from [God]. Yield yourself heartily to His will and service. Avoid an aspiring ambitious, ostentatious, assuming, arrogant, scornful, stubborn, wilful, levelling, self-justifying behavior; and strive for more and more of the humble spirit that Christ manifested while He was on earth. . . .

Humility is a most essential and distinguishing trait in all true piety. . . . It is the ornament of the spirit; the source of some of the sweetest exercises of Christian experience; the most acceptable sacrifice we can offer to God; the subject of the richest of His promises; . . . the spirit which He will crown with glory in heaven hereafter.

Earnestly seek, then, and diligently and prayerfully cherish, an humble spirit, and God shall walk with you here below; and when a few more days shall have passed, He will receive you to the honors bestowed on His people at Christ's right hand.[2]

Questions for Individuals or Groups

1. How is a healthy pride in our skills related to a healthy view of self (Gal 6:4)?

2. What is good and what is bad in taking pride in others, like family, friends, associates, your church, people who you have won to Christ (2 Cor 7:4)?

3. In what areas of your own experience have you preferred easy illusions about yourself over painful truths?

4. When is positive thinking helpful and biblical, and when is it dangerous?

5. Read Genesis 3:1-5. How does the enemy feed Eve's pride?

6. How does your vision of God affect your tendency to have pride?

7. First decide where you struggle most with pride. (You might be helped by the section "The Faces of Pride.") Then describe how a radical commitment to humility would change you (Phil 2:4-8).

8. How deeply have you understood the sinfulness of human nature? How does this affect pride? What does grace mean?

9. How can the structure of a local church help with overcoming pride for leaders?

How can pride manifest itself still in your favorite church structure?

How would you guard yourself as a leader?

9
Overcoming the Dragon Master

Entering Christ's Victory

My earliest childhood memories are of Britain at war. I can remember waking in fear to the sound of air-raid sirens wailing in the night. I remember fear on my parents' faces as they hurried us children to the shelter at the end of the street. I remember the dull thuds of distant falling bombs and the strange shrieks of flying metal that followed. I remember walking home past houses which had burned down after being hit by incendiary bombs. I remember how my parents straightened their backs as they took courage from Winston Churchill's defiant speeches over the radio. I remember hating Hitler with all my childish heart.

Many people today are more ignorant than we were as children. They stand in the midst of a war but see no enemy. Around them the battlefield evidences the terrible devastation of spiritual warfare, but they seem more puzzled than convinced. Unfortunately, in a time of war such people are often the first casualties, for the first rule of warfare is *know your enemy.*

Behind every dragon we have faced together in this book lies the malicious mind of the Dragon Master. It is no accident that you are attacked by dragons working together. It is no mere chance that they come at your weakest moments and attack your least defensible areas. They are guided by a dark intelligence, the Father of Lies, the Prince of the Power of the Air, the Accuser, the Destroyer. The king of the dragons is the Enemy.

Prime Time Evil: War

One of the silliest beliefs of our secular age is the naive confidence that all of us are basically good, that at the core of our human nature we are uncorrupted. Yet the twentieth century is the bloodiest in world history. The madness in the mud of World War 1 exterminated a whole generation of European youth. Yet within a generation Nazi power plunged the world once more into destruction, and some twenty million people died in consequence. Six million Jews were slaughtered as the deliberate policy of a nation whose civilization had been the pride of Europe.

Much of the world looked to the Russian revolution as a fresh beginning for the future of humankind. Within ten years it elevated the monster Stalin to supreme power, and in the purges that followed some twenty million people lost their lives. Communism came to Asia too, brought by Mao Zedong. During the continual conflicts of his revolutionary experiments more millions died. In little Cambodia Pol Pot sought to outdo Mao in the purity of revolution and wiped out a third of his nation in the process.

In Africa Idi Amin ruled by murder, rape, torture and terror and even now threatens a return to power in the once happy land of Uganda. Papa Doc Duvalier led Haiti into a similar horror. Although the list is only a partial one, the point is clear: We humans are in no way innately good. The book *Modern Times* tells us that almost two hundred million people have been killed in this century for political reasons.

The first step in the education of the naive secularist is to realize the wickedness of which the human heart is capable. Some try to avoid this conclusion, hoping to point the finger of blame at some aspect of humanity rather than admit the blame of the whole race. The ready targets are the institutions of society. It is the state that is at fault. Sweep it away in revolution!

No one doubts it—institutions *are* corrupted. The wickedness of antisemitism was embedded in the Nazi state, for example. The evil of racism is integral to the apartheid state of South Africa and even in the tribal despotism of Black Africa. Nor is it difficult to spot greed and materialism in our own society, or the cruelty of a vicious bureaucracy in the Soviet system. We *do* live in a corrupt society with corrupted institutions. The question is, Why is it so?

Behind each corrupt system lie people who create it and use it. Hitler made clear in his book *Mein Kampf* that he wanted to kill Jews. Hitler corrupted the system. It was not the other way around. Furthermore, carrying out his policy took the willing hands of men and women to herd Jews into the gas chambers, to insert the gas phials, to lock the doors, to steal the gold from the teeth of the dead, to torture in pseudoscientific experiments, to work people to death in slave camps, to gun them down into open grave pits and to turn a blind eye while it all happened. Institutions do indeed generate a collective power for evil, but willingly involved and cooperating at every turn are people.

Where did such evil begin? How is it all orchestrated? Who corrupted the first man? The Christian answer is both obvious and profound. Behind evil lies a dark, intelligent spirit who works within all the evil people and the evil systems. Christianity takes evil seriously and cuts through the helpless naiveté of the modern mind.

Scott Peck, a psychiatrist who with unusual honesty tried to understand the genuine wickedness of some of his more antisocial patients, finally concluded that an intelligent source of evil was present in their lives, enslaving them. He went even further:

> I wrote around and let it be known that I was interested in purported cases of possession for evaluation. Referrals trickled in. The first two cases turned out to be standard psychiatric disorders as I suspected. . . . The third turned out to be the real thing.
>
> Since then I have also been deeply involved in another case of genuine possession. In both cases I was privileged to be present at their successful exorcism.
>
> I now know Satan is real. I have met it.[1]

Meet the Enemy

Scripture does not tell us where the Enemy came from. We can, however, deduce two things about him. First, he is not eternal. Only God is "from everlasting to everlasting." The Enemy is not equal with God. He is a created being. Second, since God creates only good, the Enemy too was created good. He must have rebelled at some point, for he was not created evil. Like human beings, the Enemy was created free to choose to obey or to rebel.

When God created the world, it was his plan to restore a universe in which a Fall had already occurred. The Creator knew this creature we call the Enemy and his intentions for the human race. There were no surprises for God in all that happened. But

we need to know this Enemy well if we want to escape his dragonish snares. Who is he?

The Enemy is a liar. He was almost powerless in this new
creation of the earth. In Genesis we find that he had no power
to compel, but he did have the power of the lie. And by lying
he persuaded and trapped Eve. The essence of his lie was to
convince her that God is evil and threatened by his own creatures. "God knows that when you eat of it your eyes will be
opened, and you will be like God, knowing good and evil" (Gen
3:5).

The lie is subtle in that it contains a kernel of truth. But it
slanders God's motivation in denying the couple the fruit of one
tree. The dragon implies that God was withholding something
desirable from her because he wanted to limit her.

Now the Enemy is careful in his wording, for he knows that
Adam and Eve have great power. Under God they were given the
lordship of the world. That was symbolically conveyed when he
had them name the animals. (The act implied the bestowing of
their natures and so indicated their participation in God's creation.)

In the universe the Enemy was subservient and helpless *except
for the lie.* If the lie had been rejected, humanity would perhaps
have become the basis for God's remaking of the fallen cosmos
at once. But we are speculating here, because our first parents
did, in fact, buy the lie. What we know from Scripture is that
humanity, fallen as we are, is to be the raw material for restoring
the universe at some later date. "The creation waits in eager
expectation for the sons of God to be revealed. For the creation
was subjected to frustration, not by its own choice, but by the
will of the one who subjected it, in hope that the creation itself
will be liberated from its bondage to decay and brought into the
glorious freedom of the children of God" (Rom 8:19-21). God's

glory is revealed when he carries out his healing using the fallen sons and daughters of Eve.

We learn our first clue to the Enemy's character in his using the lie. Jesus called him "a liar and the father of lies" (Jn 8:44). Every lie is intended to pull people away from God by attacking God's character and turning his goodness into evil. It is the Enemy's fight for survival, for in the coming world where people choose obedience he will be destroyed.

This is why lying and illusion have been such a major part of this book. In one way or another they are used by every dragon. It is also why teaching the truth of God's Word is so vital and so potent a weapon against the dragons.

The most complete form of the lie is false religion where in the end Satan is worshiped. Paul tells how such things can happen: "Satan himself masquerades as an angel of light. It is not surprising, then, if his servants masquerade as servants of right-eousness" (2 Cor 11:15). Disguises are the name of the game.

The Enemy is an accuser. Once humans had fallen into rebel-lion, the Enemy gained authority. His next move was to attempt to use God against us. "Divide and rule" is his motto, and his survival depends on separating us from God. He does this by accusing us of being rebels (once he has persuaded us to rebel). Of course, our sins do lend legitimacy to his complaints about us!

The Enemy has been granted the right to accuse us before our Creator. And that is what he is busy about. He constantly points out every flaw in us, every act of meanness, every slip into cruelty or selfishness. These sins wound God because he loves us. The accusations must turn the knife in the wound. Part of God's incredible patience is that, down through the centuries of the human story, he has waited for our response to his love.

Now we can understand the joy in heaven when the Enemy

is finally dealt with:

> And there was war in heaven. Michael and his angels fought against the dragon, and the dragon and his angels fought back. But he was not strong enough, and they lost their place in heaven. The great dragon was hurled down—that ancient serpent called the devil or Satan, who leads the world astray. He was hurled to the earth, and his angels with him.
>
> Then I heard a loud voice in heaven say:
>
> "Now have come the salvation and the power and the kingdom of our God,
>
> and the authority of his Christ.
>
> For the accuser of our brothers,
>
> who accuses them before our God day and night,
>
> has been hurled down." (Rev 12:7-10)

The Enemy is a destroyer. As the Bible moves forward from the Garden of Eden, the descriptions of Satan change. In the garden he is just a whispering snake, but by the time we reach Revelation he is "the great dragon." Before the Fall, Adam had the authority over the world, but afterward that power belonged to the Enemy. And in the process humankind was enslaved by the dragon. This is why Jesus announced that he had come to set the prisoners free (Lk 4:18).

There is no question about it: The Enemy now has real power in the world today. He is responsible for the evil we find all around us, for he uses his power for destruction. In the last analysis Satan can only spoil and destroy. He cannot create. Only God does that. Satan uses all his energy and authority in the world to smash and destroy.

Sometimes people want to blame God for the evil nature of the world. But the world is evil because humans gave Satan power over it. Wherever there is disorder and confusion, wherever there is suffering and pain, there we see his dirty dragon prints. Walk through the hospital wards, look at children suffering from cancer or genetic diseases, and there you see what he enjoys doing. He is vicious and malevolent. And he is powerful partly because we have contributed to his power.

The Enemy is a tyrant. By freely choosing evil we human beings continue to sell ourselves into slavery. Time and again in these pages we have noted the hard struggle against deeply ingrained habits that are self-destructive. These are the tools of the Enemy's despotic rule over us.

I am not saying that it is legitimate to use the excuse that "the devil made me do it." We do it all too willingly! There is no escaping personal responsibility. But our sin accomplishes much more for evil than we imagine because in sinning we cooperate with and contribute to the destruction of the world.

The power that maintains our slavery to evil and damaging habits is our own stubborn rebellion against God. This has not changed since Eve's day. In striving for our own godhood we forge our own chains. It is hardly fair to blame God for the damage!

The Enemy is a murderer. I remember Marie. She was almost starving. She came to me one day at the suggestion of her husband who desperately wanted to help her. Her clothes were old and dirty, and she was living in a hovel at the back of a bar. She sold herself for what little food she ate. Her life had became a story of abuse and suffering.

It had not always been like this. Marie had once had a good home with a loving husband and two delightful children, but she liked to party. Soon her men friends led her into drugs and drunkenness, and she began to go downhill. She left her home, abandoning the children, and gave herself full-time to her wild life. Now Marie was pleading for help from the gutter.

The church found her a home and located a job. Soon she was

clean and becoming healthy, and it even looked as if her marriage might be saved. Then the family she was staying with left for a few days. When they came back Marie was gone. Neighbors reported that there had been a wild party at the house. As it turned out, some men Marie had met at her new job had begun to reclaim her for her old life, and old acquaintances had encouraged the process.

She called me once to tell me that it was no use trying to find her. She asked me to pass on a final good-by to her husband and children. She was a lost soul. I don't expect her to live long. The great dragon is a murderer.

The Place of the Fight

Satan's power in this world holds terrible sway, but we must always remember that it is limited. This is still God's world, and it remains beautiful in spite of all that we and the Enemy do. God has set severe limits on the destruction.

Our world has become a battleground in the cosmic warfare between good and evil. In the conflict God always fights consistently with his nature. He respects the freedom and dignity of those he made, even in their tragic state, and his weapons are the weapons of love and grace and goodness. Satan too is consistent. He always cheats, always lies, always enslaves and always ends up destroying life. Both their goals and the way they fight reflect the respective natures of the Lord of the universe and the Rebel.

The human heart is the battlefield. Because the warfare is spiritual, its greatest focus is in human lives, especially the lives of Christians. When God made you his, he created within you a new spiritual nature. The "old you" is still there with its bias for evil and its old habits, but deeper inside is a "new you" with a desire to live for Jesus in goodness, truth and love.

The struggle between good and evil comes down to the

choices you make—whether to live in the new you and fight for righteousness, or to live in the old you and work with evil.

Put to death, therefore, whatever belongs to your earthly nature: sexual immorality, impurity, lust, evil desires and greed, which is idolatry. . . . You used to walk in these ways, in the life you once lived. But now you must rid yourselves of all such things as these: anger, rage, malice, slander, and filthy language from your lips. Do not lie to each other, since you have taken off your old self with its practices and have put on the new self, which is being renewed in knowledge in the image of its Creator. (Col 3:5, 7-10)

You are the battlefield. The dragons are outside and inside, but it is you they are after.

The church is the battlefield. The fellowship of Christians is an outpost of heaven on earth. The people of God, his church, exists therefore in two dimensions, the first earthly and the second spiritual. This spiritual arena has become a prime field of conflict between Satan and the kingdom of God. Paul writes, "Our struggle is . . . against the spiritual forces of evil in the heavenly realms" (Eph 6:12).

The Enemy concentrates on church life, aiming to destroy it. The warfare is intense because failure here devastates not just the Christians involved, but ripples out to make of the church a mockery among people of the world. Immorality in the pastorate, ambition, factionalism, self-righteousness, legalism, false doctrine—all these weapons the Enemy deploys in the church to divide and discourage those whom God has redeemed.

The world is the battlefield. The church's task is nothing less than reclaiming the world's territory in the name of Jesus. For example, we are to take over the disarray in what God instituted as marriage and restore it as the holy example he made it to be. We are to reclaim marriage in the name of Jesus.

As we go to work in the world, we go as Christians. Our job is to reclaim work for the kingdom. God instituted it as our authority over the garden. The slithering dragon ruined the garden and our work in it, but God wants to reign in the realm of work again.

The same is true of friendship, study, research, parenting. All are areas for us to reclaim in the name of Jesus. We cannot opt out of the world. We are here to reclaim it. We are the bridge-head for a coming revolution when all the world will be his, when he returns.

This piecemeal advance into the world is disputed at every step. The great dragon and the people he has subjugated will always resent and attack Christians on the offense. This is part of the struggle.

But in the midst of abuse and rejection we are to proceed with banners of love into the battlefield, doing what is right for his sake.

As servants of God we commend ourselves in every way: in great endurance; in troubles, hardships and distresses; in beatings, imprisonments and riots; in hard work, sleepless nights and hunger; in purity, understanding, patience and kindness; in the Holy Spirit and in sincere love; in truthful speech and in the power of God; with weapons of righteousness in the right hand and in the left; through glory and dishonor, bad report and good report; genuine, yet regarded as impostors; known, yet regarded as unknown; dying, and yet we live on; beaten, and yet not killed; sorrowful, yet always rejoicing; poor, yet making many rich; having nothing, and yet possessing everything. (2 Cor 6:4-10)

What a magnificent heritage we have! The fight is on in our generation, and we have both the privilege of participating and the promise of victory.

The Decisive Battle

God's way of fighting the great battle is extraordinary, certainly not like any earthly general's offensive. Because he wants a victory of love and not power, he fights in weakness. He began his push to victory, after all, by introducing his Son into the world as a baby—hardly the way to enter a battlefield!

As Jesus grew up he began to show us what human life was meant to be. He alone kept God's law perfectly. Peter, who lived close to him for at least three years, said flatly, "He committed no sin, and no deceit was found in his mouth" (1 Pet 2:22). He drove the religious leaders to confront him, and when they did condemn him, they proved by their methods (lying) and their goal (murder) that they had been infiltrated by the Enemy. They were on the wrong side in the conflict.

Jesus stood alone and innocent before the majesty of Roman law. He stood silent, in chosen weakness. And Roman law washed its hands of him, proclaimed him innocent yet sent him out to be crucified. The Enemy gathered his power around him, stripped him, beat him and nailed him to a cross. Alone and apparently helpless, he died. In his last words Jesus let us know that even the Father had turned from him as he made his complete identification with human sin. And the Enemy danced with delight at the wound in God's heart, as Father and Son separated. God became alienated from himself for our sake.

When it was all over, friends laid him in a borrowed tomb. And the Enemy celebrated, howling his joy at the night sky. He had won at last.

Or so it seemed.

But God's ways of fighting are different, and he specializes in bringing victories out of tombs. So the wild celebration in hell's banqueting hall was interrupted by a new and final declaration. Jesus had risen!

Out from the tomb he stepped, vigorous, alive. He had taken on the last weapon of the Enemy. Death broke its power on his defenseless head and itself was shattered forever. Satan was defeated.

Now the Son stands before the Father, for you. At each accusation against you, Jesus displays his hands and side and declares you covered by his sacrifice. He intercedes for you, and Satan is silenced.

One day Jesus will return. The Enemy will flee before him and the battle will be over. Then all that mighty company from every generation, who have been set free by his victory, will sing in a voice of thunderous joy, "Worthy is the Lamb, who was slain, to receive power and wealth and wisdom and strength and honor and glory and praise!" (Rev 5:12). And all will be at peace.

The Present Struggle

In the meantime the struggle continues. Although it is only a mopping-up operation, it still can be intense. In this struggle we cannot win any victory of our own. We are instead to enter into his victory. The saints in Revelation 5, for example, overcome the dragon by the blood of the Lamb. Paul's advice for the Christian warrior is "be strong in the Lord and in *his* mighty power" (Eph 6:10).

Jesus Christ has won the decisive battle. It is over. All we are to do is to enter his victory. In his name we can defeat the enemy; by Jesus' authority we can drive evil back, and by Jesus' power we can overcome. So the vital question for holy living is this: Will I resist all temptation to rely on my own strength? Will I humbly accept his victory as the key to my freedom from whatever sin haunts me? The only way to overcome temptation is to submit myself to Jesus.

Christian warfare begins with my helplessness. I have to come to him in need of his healing touch, confessing my weakness and sin and throwing myself on his mercy. As I receive his forgiveness, he removes me to safe ground, to territory he has conquered. There and there alone I can be victorious.

This is why prayer is necessary for overcoming the dragons. In prayer we take our stand with him, and his victory mantle covers us. Victory over the dragons and over the Dragon King comes from our King. We too have to fight from weakness, leaning on him.

Once we stand on resurrection ground, the key is to stay there. "Take your stand against the devil's schemes. . . . Put on the full armor of God, so that when the day of evil comes, you may be able to stand your ground, and after you have done everything, to stand. Stand firm then" (Eph 6:11, 13-14).

The Enemy's strategy is to tempt you away from this secure ground. He will try to lure you to sleepy passivity or to attempt private battle with him alone. To resist his pull you need careful balance.

Reject pious passivity. The fact that your stand is on the ground of Jesus' victory does not mean you now sit back and rest. Standing does take effort. The whole tendency of my flesh nature, the "old me," is to draw me away from resurrection territory.

This is why self-discipline is important for the Christian. The disciplines of prayer, Bible study, church fellowship and servanthood are all part of *standing*. Train your will through the exercise of spiritual disciplines. As you do practice them, the Enemy will flee: "Submit yourselves, then, to God. Resist the devil, and he will flee from you" (Jas 4:7).

There is no flavor of "let go and let God" in that advice. Pious passivity is doomed to failure. Submission to God is an active business of the will. Yet all this emphasis on the will and on fighting is also dangerous. Keep in mind the balance necessary.

Refuse independent activism. The danger is that in rejecting passivity we might decide that merely standing is not enough, that we need to do something more than depend on Jesus. Enthusiastically determined to defeat the Enemy, we then engage him on our own. At this point spiritual pride has come into play, and we are helpless to resist him. To avoid this danger the Bible encourages a healthy awareness of the Enemy's power. Even the archangel Michael did not attack the devil on his own authority but said, "The Lord rebuke you!" (Jude 9).

I have met Christians who became overinvolved in struggles with the demonic. This is highly dangerous because, when we seek out the battle, we are probably operating on the wrong ground.

So stand. Don't race off attacking in places of your own choosing. When the Enemy attacks you on kingdom territory, your victory is certain. Even in those rare cases where he attacks you in the open, instead of through your temptations, if you stand on Jesus' ground you cannot fail. Why try to launch out on your own against so wily an Enemy when in Jesus you have guaranteed success?

Entering His Victory

"Standing" means consciously choosing to see yourself as a new person in Christ and behaving that way. Satan's aim is to persuade you to see yourself as the "old person." He wants you to really believe that *that* is you. This is his way of attack when he has you on the battlefield within.

"You, a new person?" he will scoff. "How ridiculous!" He will not fail to point out all your failures and defects. If you accept the failures as proof that you do not belong to Jesus, you will have fallen into the trap; for you belong to Jesus even when you fail. Jesus has declared you are his own, not because you are good but because he is forgiving. On the other hand, if you attempt to deny your failures, you will be caught in the lies of self-justification—and the devil will have won a round.

The answer is to apply the victory of Jesus. You take Jesus' authority and confront the Enemy. "You have no right to accuse me! It is not your business. My failures are covered and Jesus accepts me." When you take the authority of Jesus, Satan has no recourse but to flee. You drive him away when you know and claim the truth.

He will come back, of course. But each time you take hold of your authority in Christ, you will become more sure in its use. Ironically, you will grow stronger through your reliance on Christ.

The Enemy often makes serious mistakes at this point and seems to panic. His attacks may take on a tinge of the ridiculous. When you learn a little humility, for example, he will counter by accusing you of being proud of your humility! Never argue with him at such moments. Laugh that we are like that, and hold yourself firmly in Jesus' grace. Satan hates the holy laughter of God's people. It sounds like the knell of his doom. (Besides, he is very pompous.)

The devil adapts his purpose and method when the battlefield is the church. Here, where Jesus has set love as the mark of his people, his aim is to separate and divide. Here he sends the Dragon of the Tongue most effectively.

The battle now is not just to see myself "in Christ," but to see my fellow Christians as they are in him rather than as they are in the flesh. This does not mean being blind to their sin, but it does mean viewing it with the compassion Jesus has for his erring sheep.

"Standing" on the battlefield of the church means being determined to behave with generous love in every situation. If the

Enemy has lured one Christian to disparage or hurt another, we must all rally in love to enable the hurt Christian to continue to love. If he succeeds in breaking one of us, it is vital that the rest refuse to respond. Love will cover the other's offense and, in the end, squelch the dragon's fire.

The third sphere of battle is the world. We have been commissioned to reclaim it bit by bit for our King, but the dragon will challenge that we are now on his territory. That claim is false!

The world belongs to Jesus, and we exercise his authority when we claim it as resurrection ground. Once again our only power is in his name. Using the name of Jesus is your birthright as a Christian.

Fully Equipped

Paul has given careful attention in Ephesians 6 to the equipment we wear as we take our stand for resistance. The Lord has given us armor and weapons against the Enemy. We will look at three key parts of the Christian armor.

The breastplate of righteousness. This has been a book about holy living. While it may not sound as spectacular as other areas of the Christian life, about half the New Testament is aimed at encouraging holy living.

Breastplates are basic protection, covering the breast. You will never defeat Satan without yours. Check it out again. How are you doing in growth toward right living? Keep fighting the little sins and the small hypocrisies. Keep a short account with God by confessing your failures each day, renewing your determination to turn from the sin. Continue to make righteousness your aim, and your breastplate will maintain its sheen.

The shield of faith. The arrows of the Enemy are the doubts he wants to plant in you about your Lord. He wants you to fear that

God may let you down. He wants you to doubt whether God could ever really love you. These are slurs on God's character. Live close to the cross and you will not be deceived by them. "He who did not spare his own Son, but gave him up for us all—how will he not also, along with him, graciously give us all things?" (Rom 8:32).

Keep faith with Jesus. The more you know him, the more you will trust him. Infinitely faithful, he will never let you down. Let your trust in him become a mighty shield.

The sword of the Spirit. The sword of the Spirit is the Word of God. You must have noticed how often I have pressed Scripture into your hands. Let me confess my strategy. I have been trying to get you used to using the Word as a weapon, just as Jesus did in his time of temptation (read Matthew 4).

All you know of the spiritual life comes from his Word. It is truth. When the struggle is on and you are fighting for your life, the Word is your weapon.

The Lord of the Rings is J. R. R. Tolkien's masterpiece fantasy that tells the truth about the battle between good and evil. In it, the elven friends of hobbits Frodo and Samwise give Frodo a phial of light for their protection. Later the two hobbits are trapped in the lair of Shelob, the huge and foul spider that guards the way to the evil land of Mordor. When Sam comes upon the monster bending over his beloved Frodo lying unconscious, he faces her alone.

Slowly he raised his head and saw her, only a few paces away, eyeing him, her beak drabbling a spittle of venom, and a green ooze trickling from below her wounded eye. There she crouched, her shuddering belly splayed upon the ground, her great bows of her legs quivering, as she gathered herself for another spring. . . .

"Now come, you filth!" [Sam] cried. "You've hurt my master, you brute, and you'll pay for it. . . ."

As if his indomitable spirit had set its potency in motion, the glass [phial] blazed suddenly like a white torch in his hand. It flamed like a star that leaping from the firmament sears the dark air with intolerable light. No such terror out of heaven had ever burned in Shelob's face before. . . . She fell back beating the air with her forelegs, her sight blasted by inner lightnings, her mind in agony. Then turning her maimed head away, she rolled aside and began to crawl, claw by claw, towards the opening in the dark cliff behind. . . . She reached the hole, and squeezing down, leaving a trail of green-yellow slime, she slipped in, even as Sam hewed a last stroke at her dragging legs. . . .

Shelob was gone.[2]

Let the Word of God be your sword of blazing light, the phial for your protection and offense. Study it every day. Hide it in your memory. And when the enemy attacks, use it!

The dragons we face are powerful and bent on devouring us, led by the King of the dragons. But our Lord has not left us defenseless and has, in fact, assured our victory as we wield the weapons he has provided. Let us stand in full armor—and fight in the Spirit.

Questions for Individuals or Groups

1. Where did the "naive confidence that all of us are basically good" come from historically?

2. Read Romans 8:19-21 and Genesis 3:14-19. How should you view suffering and sickness in the light of these passages?

3. What is the Devil's role in God's plan? How is it linked to human freedom to choose?

4. Where did the Enemy gain his power in the world?

5. How does the Enemy use his power now? How is this related to the unfairness of life?

6. How will God vindicate his righteousness in view of all this?

7. Should we rejoice in contemplating the Enemy's end? Why (Rev 20:7-10)?

8. What is your authority in fighting Satan? How do you use it (Rom 8:33-34)?

Notes

Chapter 1: Overcoming Guilt
[1]Augustine, *Confessions*, bk. 8.

Chapter 8: Overcoming Pride
[1]Jonathan Edwards, *Charity and Its Fruits* (London: Banner of Truth, 1978), p. 132.
[2]Ibid., p. 155.

Chapter 9: Overcoming the Dragon Master
[1]M. Scott Peck, *People of the Lie* (New York: Simon & Schuster, 1983), p. 183.
[2]J. R. R. Tolkien, *The Two Towers* (New York: Houghton-Mifflin, 1967), p. 339.